TABLE OF CONTENTS

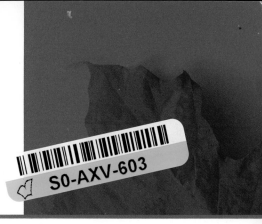

Introduction
First Nations, Métis and Inuit Children and Youth: Time to Act

Chapter 1
A Burgeoning Population:
Demographics of Aboriginal Children and Youth

Chapter 2
Income: Aboriginal Children and Youth in Need

EXECUTIVE SUMMARY

First Nations, Métis and Inuit Children and Youth: Time to Act provides a portrait of Aboriginal peoples from the perspective of the communities and social connections on which children and youth depend. This report also provides examples of what is working and recommendations for the way forward.

The approach adopted in this report is somewhat non-traditional for the National Council of Welfare. It is, however, consistent with renewed efforts to provide people affected by poverty and working to resolve it with ways to be heard. Each chapter, therefore, provides a selection of statistical highlights—or lowlights as is too often the case—and excerpts from interviews with Aboriginal women and men working with and on behalf of Aboriginal children and youth. In some places you will see the words of youth themselves. The style of the interview text is often different than the rest in an attempt to keep it as conversational as possible. In this way, readers have the sense of actually listening to people speaking. The interviewees recount their own experience in their own way and we have been guided by them rather than the reverse.

Each chapter in this report links to the others— when you read the education chapter, for example, you will not be able to "set aside" education and move on to the next topic. The issues and challenges are entwined, as is reality. The report, despite some limitations, highlights distinctions among First Nations, Métis and Inuit peoples. It also addresses differences between women and men and diversity across urban, rural, reserve and remote locations.

What the Introduction and Chapter 1 reveal about Aboriginal children and youth is the story of a rapidly growing population, one with a much greater proportion of children and youth than the non-Aboriginal population, but one that bears the legacy of historical disadvantage and exclusion. A portrait of challenges and barriers is revealed, which are added on top of the ones that other Canadian children and youth also face. The poverty and inequality that Aboriginal peoples face is largely the story of the struggle to overcome oppression – the colonialism, forced assimilation attempts, and other forms of systemic racism that have roots far into the past.

Chapters 2 and 3 focus on the economic context of children's lives. Aboriginal incomes are improving, but the gap between Aboriginal and non-Aboriginal incomes continues to widen, even under strong economic conditions. Inequalities in employment continue to impact Aboriginal children and youth whether as dependants or as young women and men participating in the labour force. Chapter 4 shows that from early learning through post-secondary education, Aboriginal young people face lack of access to education and other opportunities and the erosion of family ties, culture and language that could help them grow up with confidence and self-esteem.

Chapters 5 and 6 demonstrate how Aboriginal children and youth are at higher risk across almost all indicators of wellness and that their health cannot be disassociated from that of their families, communities and living conditions. Aboriginal housing on-reserve and elsewhere, whether in urban areas or the North, is substandard and inadequate at rates disproportionate to that of the non-Aboriginal population; homelessness is also more prevalent.

Chapters 7 and 8 look at particular consequences of a system that has gone wrong. Despite the devastating impacts of the past removal of Aboriginal children to residential schools, incredible numbers of children are still being taken into care by child welfare authorities. Many Aboriginal children "in care" graduate to the justice system where Aboriginal young women, in particular, are too often victims of crime and where Aboriginal peoples are overrepresented among youth in conflict with the law and in prison.

While in each chapter there are examples of the kinds of policies and programs that are working and some of our interviewees make specific suggestions, the National Council of Welfare, in the final section, makes two sets of recommendations. The first encourages Canadians:

- to build understanding and support for Aboriginal peoples;

- to challenge assumptions and take a stand against racism; and

- to make sure that our political leaders know we want action to improve Aboriginal lives.

The NCW also directs a set of recommendations to the federal, and other, governments, including:

- the adoption of a comprehensive national anti-poverty strategy and within it a specific vision and accountability to First Nations, Métis and Inuit peoples, and women and men equally;

- immediate investment in meeting the basic needs of children and youth;

- immediate increases in investment in programs and policies that are working or show promise;

- greater effort to build fair, sustainable governance frameworks, setting aside intergovernmental wrangling and adopting comprehensive negotiated agreements, all in the interests of a better quality of life for all Aboriginal women, men and children.

The time to act is now.

Dear Readers,

This National Council of Welfare report on First Nations, Métis and Inuit children and youth was written to show solidarity with Aboriginal demands for action, to help Canadians better understand and support needed changes, and to urge governments to act without delay in new and bold ways to give poverty-stricken Aboriginal children and youth a decent chance in life. The NCW is not an Aboriginal organization but it does know poverty and knows how severely it afflicts Aboriginal peoples.

We have tried to be as holistic as possible, to weave together the many, interconnected issues that girls and boys and young women and men face . . . whether they are First Nations, Métis or Inuit and whether they live in urban or rural areas, on reserves or settlements, or Northern and Arctic regions. This is a non-traditional report for the NCW as we have also combined statistical examples of the desperate need for change with an emphasis on the voices of Aboriginal people. This helps give true meaning to the numbers.

We do not hide the grim reality that growing up as an Aboriginal child or young person too often entails. But we also want to bring to light the ways in which Aboriginal people themselves are making things better, despite the odds. There are programs and policies that are working. And many more that could work . . . if only other Canadians and Canadian governments would do the right and smart thing by supporting and investing in them.

On behalf of the current Council and staff, I want to thank everyone involved in this project, starting with the participants at a 2005 roundtable that helped focus the report. Special thanks are due to the dedicated women and men who agreed to be interviewed for our report and you will be introduced to them in the next couple of pages.

Much appreciation is also owed to Aboriginal reviewers and advisors who helped guide and refine our work, including former Council members—whose commitment kept us going even after their terms ended, and former researchers. From the wealth of information provided, we had to make many difficult decisions about what to include within the confines of this one report. Finally, we are indebted to the passionate collaboration of our writer who pulled it all together. You will find all their names at the end of the report, along with current Council members and staff.

…/2

112, RUE KENT STREET, 9th FLOOR/9e ÉTAGE | PLACE DE VILLE, TOWER/TOUR B | OTTAWA, ONTARIO K1A 0J9
613-957-2961 | FAX/TÉLÉCOPIEUR 613-957-0680 | www.ncwcnbes.net

National Council
of Welfare

Conseil national
du bien-être social

As Council members, we are frankly astounded at the patience and good faith of Aboriginal peoples. Our own discussions during the research and writing of this report made us increasingly impatient, frustrated and angry.

Our recommendations reflect this impatience. We are a rich country. We have choices. We can choose to provide Aboriginal children and youth with a much better chance in life. But it is way too late for small, timid steps. We need big, bold, innovative, forward thinking, including a national anti-poverty strategy that is built by, for and with Aboriginal peoples.

John Rook
Chairperson

Cindy Blackstock, a member of the Gitksan First Nation, has worked in the field of child and family services for over 20 years. She is currently the Executive Director of the First Nations Child and Family Caring Society of Canada and Co Convenor for the Sub Group for the Rights of Indigenous Children and Youth.

David Budd is a Youth Cultural Worker at Ma Mawi Wi Chi Itata Centre in Winnipeg, Manitoba.

Peter Dinsdale is the Executive Director of the National Association of Friendship Centres.

Okalik Eegeesiak is the Director of the Socio-Economic Development Department of Inuit Tapiriit Kanatami.

Dr. Valerie Gideon is the Senior Director of the Assembly of First Nations' Health and Social Secretariat.

Jane Gray works with Assembly of First Nations as the National Project Manager of the First Nations Regional Longitudinal Health Survey (RHS).

Charles W. (Charlie) Hill from Six Nations is the Executive Director of the National Aboriginal Housing Association (NAHA).

Garry Jobin, a Cree, is the Coordinator of BladeRunners in Vancouver, a program that started in 1994 to match construction labour needs with disadvantaged, street-involved youth, about 95% of whom are Aboriginal and 28% female. Within two years, it was formally supported by the BC government and has a solid track record of success.

Alastair MacPhee is a consultant to the Congress of Aboriginal Peoples.

Dr. Nathan Matthew is a professional educator, long-time Chairman of the Shuswap Nation Tribal Council and is the British Columbia First Nations Representative on the Education Advisory Council to the Minister of Education. In 1987 he began directing and instructing a national course at the University of British Columbia for Principals of First Nation Schools.

Mary Jane Norris is an Aboriginal demographer and Senior Research Manager with the Strategic Research and Analysis Directorate at the federal department of Indian and Northern Affairs Canada.

Dr. Catherine (Cathy) Richardson has a PhD in Child and Youth Care. She is a counsellor and family therapist as well as an Aboriginal child welfare advocate. Dr. Richardson has conducted a research study on Metis Identity

Creation and Resistance to Colonization and Mistreatment. She has worked as an Aboriginal Early Child Development advisor and is actively involved in advancing Response-Based practice and Indigenous resistance models. As well, she is involved in community leadership, agency governance and community safety, offering her perspectives and services to agencies such as Metis Community Services in Victoria, the BC Yukon Transition House Society, the Liard Aboriginal Women's Society. She is the president of the Aboriginal Family Therapy Centre, a university instructor and community educator. Her work has centered around integrating healing and social justice, particularly to victims of violence and internees of the residential schools. Catherine Richardson is married, has three children and lives in Cowichan Bay on Vancouver Island.

Justice Murray Sinclair was appointed to the Court of Queen's Bench of Manitoba in 2001. In 1988, when he was appointed the Associate Judge of the Provincial Court of Manitoba, he was that province's first Aboriginal Judge, and at that time, Canada's second. That same year he was made Co-Commissioner of the Aboriginal Justice Inquiry to investigate the condition of Aboriginal people in all aspects of the justice system.

Maria Wilson is the Training and Development Coordinator of the Socio-Economic Development Department of Inuit Tapiriit Kanatami.

FIRST NATIONS, MÉTIS AND INUIT CHILDREN AND YOUTH: TIME TO ACT

> *Children have a special place in Aboriginal cultures. According to tradition, they are gifts from the spirit world and must be treated well or they will return to that realm.*
>
> Royal Commission on Aboriginal Peoples

Over past decades literally dozens of reports have been published on the appalling circumstances of Aboriginal children and youth in this country; notwithstanding this volume of research, the situation remains fundamentally unchanged.

And yet, the poverty-related challenges faced by Aboriginal children and youth are also faced by Canada. Existing problems related to Aboriginal child and youth poverty are only likely to increase in the future, if not adequately addressed in the present.

As shown in the different Chapters of this report, Aboriginal children and youth face many poverty-related barriers, including but not limited to income, education and culture, employment, health, housing, being taken into care and justice.

At the outset, it should be noted that there is great diversity among Aboriginal peoples, including urban and rural; status and non-status, on- and off-reserve First

Nations; Inuit; and Métis, reflected in the multiplicity of issues they face.[1] There is no single way of defining Aboriginal populations, whether by identity or by tracking ancestry.[2] The different data sources available to us therefore also use a variety of definitions and terms.

Nor is there any one "Aboriginal" view on issues, rather the diversity of viewpoints reflects that of the people.

Of the 30 million people in Canada in 2001, 976,305 Canadians reported identifying with at least one Aboriginal group, or reported themselves as being Registered or Treaty Indian, and/or having Band or First Nation membership. This population forms the basis of our report.

In addition, some Canadians reported they had Aboriginal ancestors, even though they did not report having an Aboriginal identity. With them included, the Aboriginal "ancestry" population totals over 1.3 million.

	TOTAL (All ages)	CHILDREN (0-14 years)	YOUTH (15-24 years)
TOTAL Aboriginal Identity	**976,305**	**323,955**	**169,065**
First Nations	608,850	213,530	103,755
Métis	292,305	84,695	52,265
Inuit	45,075	17,465	8,255
Multiple and other Aboriginal responses	30,080	8,280	4,795

Source: 2001 Census

In many cases, the situation of Aboriginal peoples today has roots in the history of European arrival in Canada.[3]

In the ensuing legacy of colonialism, Canada's *Constitution Act*, 1867 assigned responsibility for Indians and lands reserved for Indians to the federal government.

In 1876, the first *Indian Act* was created, based on the notion of wardship, treating Indians as minors. The Act created the status Indian and an Indian registry maintained by the federal government, as well as limited, supervised, Indian governance on-reserve.[4]

Aboriginal people not registered under the Act and/or who do not live on a reserve largely come under the same federal-provincial/territorial regimes as other Canadians. The policies and programs that affect them, however, were rarely designed to take into account Aboriginal needs and circumstances, including the experience of discrimination.

The different groups of Aboriginal peoples have different relationships to federal and provincial/territorial governments in Canada. These groups also affect the ways in which individuals are identified and counted. Aboriginal peoples include First Nations (or status and non-status Indians), Métis and Inuit.

The term Indian has its roots in colonialism and has survived due to its application to those registered under the *Indian Act* and described as status or registered Indians. Non-status Indians are those persons who lost their status as Indians for a number of reasons including military enlistment and marriage to a non-Indian man, or who were never registered or entitled to be in the first place. The term First Nations tends to be more widely used now than the term Indian. When we refer to First Nations, we include status and non-status Indians in urban centres, rural areas and on reserves.

Métis are a population of mixed ancestry that grew from early intermarriage of Aboriginal and European people and over time developed a distinct cultural identity. Only recently have the Métis been legally recognized as distinct Aboriginal peoples.

Inuit have a particular identity that is closely intertwined with geography, having lived in the northernmost parts of Canada for thousands of years and forming the majority of the population in these areas.

As noted in the 1996 Royal Commission on Aboriginal Peoples (RCAP) Report, many ghosts haunt the present day situation of Aboriginal peoples, including those of dishonoured treaties, theft of Aboriginal lands, suppression of Aboriginal cultures, abduction of Aboriginal children, and impoverishment and disempowerment of Aboriginal peoples.[5]

To date, no governmental response has made major inroads into the issues raised by RCAP. Sadly not much has changed since the report, despite a succession of agreements and publications geared towards improving the living conditions of Aboriginal children and youth.

Indeed, the Assembly of First Nations (AFN) 2006 report card gave "Fs" or "Ds" to government for delivery on most of the RCAP recommendations concerning children.[6]

In November 2005, the landmark Accord reached in Kelowna among First Ministers and National Aboriginal Leaders on Aboriginal issues was the first meaningful response to RCAP. It includes objectives, some specific targets and timelines as well as evaluation and accountability. However, the Government of Canada has not honoured this commitment.

The Council recognizes that Aboriginal peoples, particularly children and youth, are among Canadians at highest risk of poverty; accordingly, the conditions of Aboriginal children and youth are an inherent reason for the Council's call for a national anti-poverty strategy.[7]

It is with these perspectives that the Council developed this report, distinguished by the following:

- The report brings together information on many issues from a variety of sources;
- It highlights some new data and previously overlooked or underused sources;
- It is centered around extensive interviews with Aboriginal experts; and
- The report has been written with important input and consultation from individuals and organizations representing First Nations, Métis and Inuit.

Where possible, despite the somber nature of the issues and all that needs to be done, we have identified examples of success stories and promising practices.

Finally, in light of the interconnectedness of all the factors that contribute to Aboriginal child and youth poverty, we encourage readers to step back from any particular issue and consider the big picture.

CHAPTER 1

A BURGEONING POPULATION: DEMOGRAPHICS OF ABORIGINAL CHILDREN AND YOUTH

> *The success that we as a society have in enabling Aboriginal single mothers to improve their circumstances will have a major impact on Aboriginal children and on the future of Canada.*
>
> Jeremy Hull, *Aboriginal Single Mothers in Canada*

Any study of First Nations, Métis and Inuit peoples in Canada must recognize the changing demographics of the last decades. While the Canadian population as a whole is ageing at a rapid rate, the Aboriginal population is much younger.[1] Equally, the growth rate of Canada's Aboriginal population has been much higher in recent decades than that of the non-Aboriginal population.

The expansion of a youthful Aboriginal population occurring simultaneously with the ageing of the mainstream boomer population presents challenges for the childcare and education system as well as housing, but could also proffer previously unprecedented labour and employment opportunity for Aboriginal youth.

A BURGEONING YOUTHFUL POPULATION

The Aboriginal population in general is growing, representing a greater percentage of the Canadian population in 2001 than in 1996[2]; as noted above, it is also a much younger population than the mainstream.

As observed by demographer Mary Jane Norris:

> *First of all, the Aboriginal population continues to have a very youthful age structure, especially compared to the non-Aboriginal mainstream population. This younger age structure is a reflection of previously very high Aboriginal fertility rates.*

Chart 1.1 shows the contrast between the ageing of the non-Aboriginal and Aboriginal Canadian population.

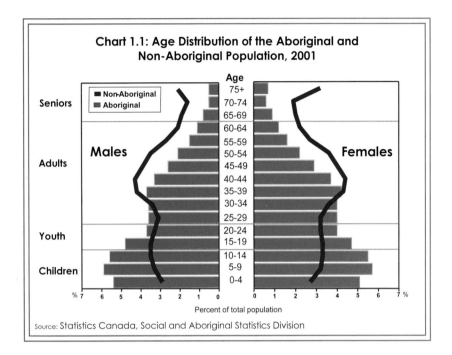

Chart 1.1: Age Distribution of the Aboriginal and Non-Aboriginal Population, 2001

Seniors

Adults

Youth

Children

Males

Females

■ Non-Aboriginal
■ Aboriginal

Age
75+
70-74
65-69
60-64
55-59
50-54
45-49
40-44
35-39
30-34
25-29
20-24
15-19
10-14
5-9
0-4

% 7 6 5 4 3 2 1 0   0 1 2 3 4 5 6 7 %

Percent of total population

Source: Statistics Canada, Social and Aboriginal Statistics Division

The Inuit population was the youngest with 57% under 25 and 39% under 15. Métis under 25 made up 47% of the total Métis population with 29% under the age of 15.[7]

In several provinces, Aboriginal children make up nearly a quarter of all children; in Saskatchewan they are 25% and in Manitoba 23%; much larger than the 14% that Aboriginal people make up of the provincial population in each province.[8]

The median[9] age of the Aboriginal population is much younger than other Canadians:

- The Aboriginal population in Canada has a median age of 24.7, ranging from 20.6 for Inuit to 27 for Métis;

- Non-Aboriginal people have a high 37.7 years median age—13 years older than the overall Aboriginal population.

- In Nunavut, the median age of the Aboriginal population is 19.1;

- In Saskatchewan, Aboriginal people have a median age of 20.1;

- In Manitoba, Aboriginal people are 22.8 years old at the median.[10]

Aboriginal children and youth account for an even larger proportion of the overall child and youth population than do Aboriginal people as a whole. While Aboriginal children under 15 were 5.6% of all children, Aboriginal people were only 3.3% of the total population.[3]

Aboriginal children under 15 made up 33% of all Aboriginal people in 2001, while children in the non-Aboriginal population only accounted for 19%.[4] Aboriginal youth aged 15-24 made up 17% of the total Aboriginal population, compared to youth making up only 13% of the non-Aboriginal population.[5]

The First Nations on-reserve population is even younger than the total Aboriginal population as 54% of all on-reserve residents were under age 25 in 2001. Of Aboriginal people not on a reserve, 49% were under age 25, and half of those lived in large cities.[6]

Statistics Canada predicts that the Aboriginal population aged 0 to 14 years will grow from 6% of all children in Canada in 2001 to over 7.4% in 2017.[11] Similarly, by 2017 the population of Aboriginal young adults (aged 20 to 29 years) will have increased from 4.1% to 5.3%.[12]

By way of further example, by 2017 in Saskatchewan, Aboriginal children are projected to form 35% of the population of all children while they will constitute 30% in Manitoba and 11% in Newfoundland and Labrador.[13]

In Saskatchewan and Manitoba, the growth of the young Aboriginal adult population from 17% and 16.6% respectively in the two provinces in 2001 to 30.3% and 23.5 % by 2017[14] will mean important changes for the composition of the young workforce.

EMERGING PRESSURES AND POSSIBILITIES

This young Aboriginal population presents important challenges for the childcare system, the education system, access to adequate housing and ultimately the labour force.

As noted by Norris,

While Aboriginal fertility levels are declining they are still relatively high, especially compared to the general population. And, while the Aboriginal population is ageing, it can be best characterized as ageing from youth into the labour force entry age groups, compared to the mainstream population which is ageing from the labour force into retirement ages.

Because of these demographic contrasts, policy issues can be expected to differ between the two populations. Many of the major concerns confronting Aboriginal people today revolve more around youth. For example, educational attainment, labour force entry and participation,

employment and unemployment are especially critical within Aboriginal populations with a high share of their population moving into the work force.

Future population growth and changes in age structure will also affect future demands for other services, such as housing, especially as the large numbers of children today become young adults of tomorrow, enter the labour force, leave home and form their own families. These trends could be expected to create new housing demands.

On the other hand, issues for the general population tend to be more focused on aspects such as retirement, labour shortages and requirements.

However, Norris reflects on these demographic differences with some optimism:

Nevertheless, these issues can be connected between the two populations, especially in smaller population provinces with significant shares of Aboriginal population. For example, in Saskatchewan where labour force shortages are a concern, the province's young Aboriginal population is projected to make up an increasing share of that province's population in the labour force age groups.

Here population growth of Aboriginal youth into labour force ages may be an opportunity to help fill future labour requirements.

However, in order for Aboriginal youth to move into this emerging labour force gap, systemic racial discrimination[15] must be addressed as an important factor; as noted in the employment Chapter, even with comparable education Aboriginal people fare poorly in the work force compared to their non-Aboriginal counterparts.

BEGINNING TO AGE

The 2001 Census noted that while Aboriginal people are much younger overall than the non-Aboriginal population, they are also beginning to age due to lengthening life expectancy and declining birth rates. The percentage of Aboriginal children under the age of 15 years as a part of the total Aboriginal population is projected to decline from 33% to 29% by 2017.[16]

As noted by Norris,

> Because of declining fertility trends and decreasing mortality trends (increasing life expectancy), the age structure of Aboriginal populations is expected to shift to older ages. Generally, greater growth is anticipated in the older age groups, such that the shares of children and youth will decrease over time. Even with increased numbers of children, greater growth in older cohorts will reduce the share of children.

While this will have consequences for growth of the Aboriginal seniors' population, it will occur much later than for the non-Aboriginal seniors' population. For example, the median age of Aboriginal people is projected to move from 24.7 years in 2001 to only 27.8 years by 2017.[17] Statistics Canada notes that the Aboriginal birth rate is still around 1.5 times that of the overall birth rate.[18]

ABORIGINAL IDENTITY: NON-DEMOGRAPHIC INFLUENCES

SELF-IDENTIFICATION

While increases in the Aboriginal population are due in part to the birth rate, they are also the result of a growing number of citizens who identified as Aboriginal in recent censuses. Aboriginal children and youth identify as First Nations, Inuit, Métis and multiple origins. Increasingly more Aboriginal people choose to identify as such, with a particularly marked growth in self-identification in the Métis population.

According to Norris,

> Ethnic mobility, including the intra- and inter-generational transmission of identity, can also affect the population growth, including that of children and youth. Analyses of Census data indicate that ethnic mobility has impacted Aboriginal population counts.

For example, the Métis population increased from 204,115 in 1996 to 292,310 in 2001.[19] Of that growth in Métis people, more than two-thirds was the result of new identification. For First Nations and Inuit the proportion was less but still very significant.

Dr. Cathy Richardson observes that due to colonial history, after 1885 (the last Federal battle against the Métis), the Métis lost their right to live as a nation and as a collective. Accordingly, many Métis went

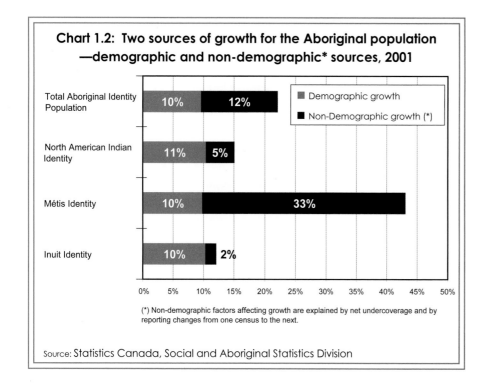

Chart 1.2: Two sources of growth for the Aboriginal population —demographic and non-demographic* sources, 2001

Total Aboriginal Identity Population: 10% Demographic growth, 12% Non-Demographic growth (*)

North American Indian Identity: 11%, 5%

Métis Identity: 10%, 33%

Inuit Identity: 10%, 2%

Legend: ■ Demographic growth ■ Non-Demographic growth (*)

(*) Non-demographic factors affecting growth are explained by net undercoverage and by reporting changes from one census to the next.

Source: Statistics Canada, Social and Aboriginal Statistics Division

underground and from that time onwards a lot of people hid their cultural identity and didn't tell their children that they were Métis:

> If you look at the Canadian census after that period, 1885 around that area, suddenly there were hardly any people who were registering as Métis although there were still many who stayed there but the numbers of people registering as French, Italian or other ethnicities went up. So basically the Métis went underground and moved westward in a kind of exodus.

Norris further highlights that this growth:

> . . . is not solely western-based. In fact, although the largest Métis population lived in Alberta in 2001 (accounting for almost 23% of the Canada's total Metis population) between 1996 and 2001 the Métis population increased in all 10 provinces, more than doubling in Ontario, New Brunswick and Nova Scotia.[20]

Inferring demographic implications from earlier under reporting, it may be that as more Aboriginal people become aware of and embrace their heritage, they increasingly self identify and the number of Aboriginal people continues to grow.

STATUS AND THE INDIAN ACT

Conversely, the registered status Indian population is in decline due to government rules governing status entitlement. In 1985, the Canadian government passed Bill C-31, amending the Indian status and band membership provisions of the Indian Act.[21]

Arising from Bill C-31, the Indian Act contains two categories of Indian registration. Pursuant to subsection 6(1), a child is registered as a status Indian where both parents of the child are or were entitled to registration, and under subsection 6(2), where one of the child's parents is or was entitled to registration under section 6(1).

Where a registered Indian father is not stated or not recognized by the government, there is a loss of benefits and entitlements by either the child or their subsequent children where there is successive out-parenting. In providing for the return of Indian status to women who lost it due to out-marriage plus their children (the second-generation cut-off), the discriminatory effect of Bill C-31 is only postponed until subsequent generations. Section 6 translates into a loss of registration after two consecutive generations of out-parenting with non-registered partners, and is anticipated to eliminate Indian status in the foreseeable future, as more First Nations persons have children with non-status people.[22]

The benefits conferred by registration are of great importance to First Nations women who remain most often the primary care givers of children. The tangible benefits attendant upon obtaining Indian registration are desirable: access/entitlement to Indian and Northern Affairs Canada's (INAC) programming base, tax benefits for those with reserve-based property, and access to national programs such as post-secondary education and non-insured health benefits. There are also additional non-tangible benefits that registration may facilitate such as personal, community and cultural identification.[23]

Registration also determines membership in bands whose lists are maintained by INAC, which in turn often determines access to band resources. A First Nations child denied registration will also be denied band membership where their band's membership list is managed by INAC. They may also be denied band membership where their band has assumed control of membership under the *Indian Act*, though this is entirely dependent upon the membership code of each First Nation.

According to Norris:

> As well, there are also other legislative (Indian Act) and identity (ethnic mobility) factors that can affect one group more than another.

Some of these factors can affect the group's population of children.

For example, the future growth of children in the registered Indian population will be affected by the 1985 provisions in the Indian Act concerning the inheritance rules and "out" marriage (exogamy). Declines in the share of children in the registered Indian population may occur through exogamous (registered, non-registered) parenting which determines the eligibility of children. After two successive generations of intermarriage, descendents are not entitled to registration and hence, no longer part of the registered Indian population.

On the other hand, these same children not entitled to registration could increasingly add to the growth in the share of the non-registered Indian population. In other words, in addition to fertility, Indian Act provisions and intermarriage can be contributing factors to the growth of children in the non-registered Indian population. These trends will also have implications for a growth of loss of entitlement privileges, such as non-insured health benefits, among children and youth.

While children can be expected to make up a growing share in the non-registered population, for the other Aboriginal groups (Métis, Inuit, registered Indian), children and youth shares are projected to decline because of declining fertility and additionally, Indian Act provisions for the registered Indian.

Not only are Aboriginal populations in flux, Aboriginal people themselves are more mobile than their non-Aboriginal counterparts, with the urban Aboriginal population moving frequently.

	TOTAL	Urban	Rural non-reserve	On-reserve
TOTAL Aboriginal Identity	**976,305**	**494,095**	**196,130**	**286,080**
First Nations	608,850	263,250	73,190	272,410
Métis	292,305	199,015	85,970	7,315
Inuit	45,075	12,195	31,070	1,810
Multiple and other Aboriginal responses	30,080	19,635	5,900	4,545

Source: 2001 Census

A POPULATION IN MOVEMENT

A major difference between the situation of many Aboriginal and non-Aboriginal people is their degree of movement. For example, Aboriginal people (not including reserve population) are nearly twice as likely to move in a given year as non-Aboriginal people.[24] About 30% of the Aboriginal population in large cities moves each year.[25]

There is much less movement in the First Nations on-reserve population who are about as likely to move as non-Aboriginal people in large cities.[26] Inuit, 86% of whom lived in the North, based on 2001 Census data, are also less mobile and most of their movement is within the same community.[27]

Most non-registered Indians (73%) and Métis (68%) live in cities. Inuit live primarily in rural, remote and fly-in communities (69%) while 49% of registered Indians live on-reserve.[28]

Norris refers to the phenomenon of high mobility as "churn":

> "Churn" refers to the very high rates of mobility and migration within urban areas, with high rates of in- and out-migration (to and from cities, between reserves and cities), and high rates of residential mobility within cities. These high rates of mobility and migration can impact in a number of ways, affecting the delivery of programs and services, and having disruptive effects on families and children. This is particularly relevant in the area of education, with indications that high mobility and change can negatively affect children's educational outcomes.

The implications of high population turnover for Aboriginal people and their communities could include:

- family instability and dissolution;
- economic marginalization;
- high victimization and crime rates;

- disruptive impacts on service delivery such as health, social and education services;

- negative impact on cultural development in urban areas; and

- weak social cohesion in Aboriginal and broader urban communities and neighbourhoods.[29]

These potential impacts are exacerbated when the family is lone parent and/or low income/high need.

LONE PARENTING: ABORIGINAL MOTHERS AND FATHERS

Aboriginal women remain most often the primary caregivers of children yet they experience lower incomes and higher rates of unemployment than Aboriginal men or other women.

Registered status Indians have twice as high a proportion of lone-mother families as other Canadians. In 1996, more than 25% of registered Indian children lived in lone-mother families, compared to 14% of non-Aboriginal children.[30] Inuit lone parenthood is not as prevalent as among other Aboriginal peoples but is higher than for non-Inuit families.[31]

Aboriginal women aged 15 to 24 years were found to be more than three times as likely to be lone mothers as the general population in that age group, with about one in three Aboriginal mothers being a lone parent.[32] While many Aboriginal women and their children experience the detrimental effects of poverty, teenage mothers and their offspring may suffer disproportionately.

On-reserve, 32% of First Nations children lived with a lone parent in 2001, as shown in Chart 1.3. In large census metropolitan areas (CMAs),18% of non-Aboriginal children lived with a lone parent contrasted with 46% of Aboriginal children.[33]

More specific 2002/03 data from the First Nations Regional Longitudinal Health Survey (RHS) indicate that almost all children living in First Nations communities (94.6%) lived with one or

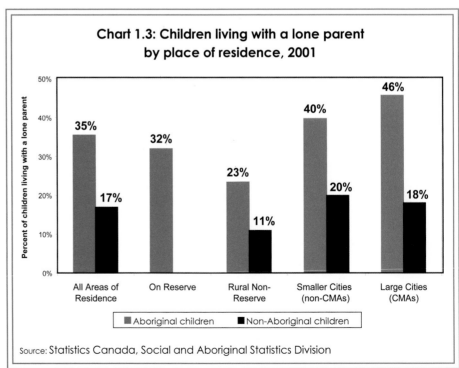

Chart 1.3: Children living with a lone parent by place of residence, 2001

Percent of children living with a lone parent

All Areas of Residence — Aboriginal: 35%, Non-Aboriginal: 17%
On Reserve — Aboriginal: 32%
Rural Non-Reserve — Aboriginal: 23%, Non-Aboriginal: 11%
Smaller Cities (non-CMAs) — Aboriginal: 40%, Non-Aboriginal: 20%
Large Cities (CMAs) — Aboriginal: 46%, Non-Aboriginal: 18%

■ Aboriginal children   ■ Non-Aboriginal children

Source: Statistics Canada, Social and Aboriginal Statistics Division

both of their parents—54.6% with two parents and 40% with one parent.[34]

In the context of Métis history, migration and lone parenthood, Dr. Richardson observed,

> So what happened, in a very short time our families moved from being what we would call extended families or living more communally in communities. But within houses too it was quite normal that grandparents might live with a family or an aunt or uncle. And so we moved from that situation maybe quite quickly to a period of a nuclear family to a time when many of our families actually now are single-parent families living in urban settings or in small resource towns, so quite vulnerable to the flux of industries and facing a lot of issues related to poverty.

Clearly, high incidences of lone parenthood impact the social and economic well being of Aboriginal children and youth who are in the lone parent's care. In addition, the plight of young Aboriginal mothers is dual: both they and their children are affected.

This critical factor has been recognized in the Indigenous Fathers' Project out of the University of Victoria. This project is the first look at Aboriginal fathers in North America, and collated interviews with 80 men of all ages and backgrounds, from lone parents to men who had never met their children.[35]

The premise of the study is that Aboriginal fathers have been over-looked as both a stakeholder group and a resource for Aboriginal children and youth. Low participation of Aboriginal fathers in infant and early childhood care has been found in research by Aboriginal communities collaborating with the study. This disassociation cannot be separated from Aboriginal men's higher rates of poverty, illness, injury and early death compared to non-Aboriginal men, as well as lower standards of housing.

The study found that:

> Among broad determinants of Aboriginal fathers' involvement with their children, one of the most significant is poverty. In the current study, although 61% of the fathers had at least some part-time work, 37.5% were living far below the poverty line . . .[36]

Aboriginal fathers have asked to be part of the research—in the words of one father:

> Just to be able to tell our stories. To shine some light on the struggle that some of us Aboriginal men have to learn what it means to be fathers and how to stay connected with our children.[37]

Carrier Sekani Grand Chief Ed John has summed it up: "Aboriginal fathers are probably the greatest untapped resource for improving the quality of life for Aboriginal children." [38]

It should also be noted that only 0.6% of non-Aboriginal children in large urban areas lived with either a relative other than their parent(s), or with a non-relative compared to almost 5% of Aboriginal children who lived with neither parent.[39] Aboriginal children are therefore between 7 and 8 times as likely as non-Aboriginal children to be raised by someone other than their parent(s). Much of this may be related also to the number of Aboriginal children in care, as discussed further in that chapter. It also reflects extended Aboriginal family structure and custom adoptions. In Inuit culture, for example, couples unable to have children could make a request to adopt from a family with several children. Traditional adoption practices have now been legally recognized by Northern governments. [40]

IN SUMMARY

Aboriginal peoples are a rapidly growing population, one with a much greater proportion of children and youth than the mainstream and Aboriginal people, other than First Nations on-reserve and Inuit, are much more likely to be mobile. Disproportionate numbers of Aboriginal children and youth are being raised in lone-parent families with all the challenges to social and economic well-being that entails.

The Aboriginal population is slowly beginning to age, but will remain significantly younger than the overall Canadian population. It is likely that the number of Aboriginal people identified as Inuit, Métis, and non-status Indians will continue to grow, and in the absence of legislative or policy change,[41] the number of status Indians will continue to decline. This decline in the registered Indian status population will translate to more First Nations people being denied the socio-economic benefits of status, a particular concern given high rates of lone parenting.

INCOME: ABORIGINAL CHILDREN AND YOUTH IN NEED

Aboriginal people in Canada endure ill health, insufficient and unsafe housing, polluted water supplies, inadequate education, poverty and family breakdown at levels usually associated with impoverished developing countries. The persistence of such social conditions in this country—which is judged by many to be the best place in the world to live—constitutes an embarrassment to Canadians, an assault on the self-esteem of Aboriginal people and a challenge to policy makers.

Royal Commission on Aboriginal Peoples, Volume 3

Aboriginal children and youth are growing up in a Canada where the gap between rich and poor is growing and where the average income of Aboriginal families and individuals continues to be far less than that of other Canadians. The income gap between men and women further affects the many Aboriginal children and youth being raised by lone mothers or other female relatives, as well as the young women themselves who are raising the next generation. Aboriginal children and youth are far more likely than other Canadian young people to live in a family, household or even a whole community that is impoverished. They are also more likely to live in deepest poverty, trying to survive on welfare incomes that fall far short of any poverty line.

THE ABORIGINAL INCOME GAP

The median[1] Canadian family income has been steadily increasing since the mid 1990s in step with a strong economy.[2] Census data show that Aboriginal people, however, had a considerably lower median income than the non-Aboriginal population in 2000. As Chart 2.1 shows, there were also large differences within the Aboriginal population for the 25-54 age group, usually considered to be peak earning years. The lowest median income was that of status Indian women. The largest gap for men is faced by status Indian men whose incomes are over $20,000 less or only 45% of non-Aboriginal men's incomes. There is also a very large gap between status and non status Indian men. Métis women and men had the highest median incomes, but their incomes were still far below those of non-Aboriginal women and men.

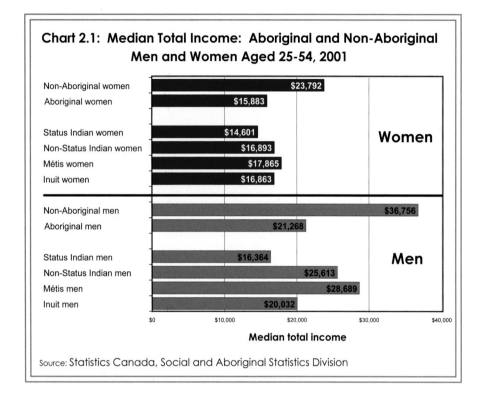

Chart 2.1: Median Total Income: Aboriginal and Non-Aboriginal Men and Women Aged 25-54, 2001

	Median total income
Non-Aboriginal women	$23,792
Aboriginal women	$15,883
Status Indian women	$14,601
Non-Status Indian women	$16,893
Métis women	$17,865
Inuit women	$16,863
Non-Aboriginal men	$36,756
Aboriginal men	$21,268
Status Indian men	$16,364
Non-Status Indian men	$25,613
Métis men	$28,689
Inuit men	$20,032

Source: Statistics Canada, Social and Aboriginal Statistics Division

With regard to Inuit women, whose median income is higher than the Aboriginal average, and for Inuit men whose income is close to the average, it is important to note that because most Inuit live in the North where the cost of living is very high, their incomes do not have the same purchasing power.

According to special data requested by Inuit Tapiriit Kanatami from the 2001 Census, Inuit incomes (for those 15 years and over) were low in all regions and substantially lower than incomes for non-Inuit living in those same regions. Inuit median income in 2000 was $13,471 and there was little variation by region:

- $12,024 in Nunatsiavut (Northern coastal Labrador);

- $13,090 in Nunavut;

- $14,384 in Inuvialuit Region (Northwest Territories);

- $14,979 in Nunavik (Northern Quebec);

- $14,150 in the rest of Canada.

Non-Inuit median income in these regions ranged from 1.5 times higher than median Inuit income in Nunavik to 3.8 times higher in Nunavut.

Looking at longer-term trends, from 1980 to 2000 the gap in median total income between Aboriginal and non Aboriginal populations aged 25-54 widened. Aboriginal people, men and women combined, had lower median income in 2000 ($18,136) than they did in 1980 ($21,400) in constant 2000 dollars.[3] The 2001 Census also showed growing disparity in income between Aboriginal and non-Aboriginal Canadians. While non-Aboriginal incomes also decreased somewhat over this 20 year period, from $31,218 to $30,023, the gap between Aboriginal and non-Aboriginal people widened to over $11,000.[4]

Comparisons over time should be interpreted cautiously due to the ethnic mobility factor discussed in Chapter 1.

More recent data derived from the Survey of Labour and Income Dynamics (SLID) examined income for both Aboriginal and non-Aboriginal persons. The data show that in 2004 median income for Aboriginal people (SLID does not include reserves or the territories) was $17,000 compared to $23,900 for non-Aboriginal persons.[5]

Again using SLID data and looking specifically at the 16-64 age group, the main labour force years for most people, Aboriginal people have been falling behind. Despite an initial increase from $14,800 in 1996 to $19,700 in 2000, median income for Aboriginal people then declined to $17,200 in 2004. Non-Aboriginal median income increased steadily reaching $25,300 by 2004, resulting in an income gap between Aboriginal and non-Aboriginal 16 to 64 year olds of 47%.[6]

These long-term and recent income trends indicate that many Aboriginal people have not benefited from economic prosperity and have actually lost ground.

THE GENDER GAP

In the Aboriginal community as among other Canadians there is a sizeable gender gap in income. As shown in Chart 2.2, Aboriginal women in every age group trail behind Aboriginal men, as well as non-Aboriginal women and men, in income.

The median income of Aboriginal women aged 25-54 in 2000 at $15,883 was approximately $8,000 less than the median income of non-Aboriginal women, as shown in Chart 2.1.[7] Women's incomes are particularly important to Aboriginal

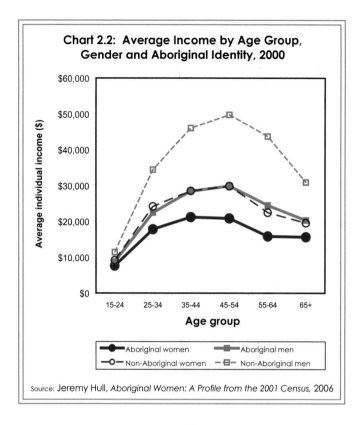

Chart 2.2: Average Income by Age Group, Gender and Aboriginal Identity, 2000

Source: Jeremy Hull, *Aboriginal Women: A Profile from the 2001 Census*, 2006

families, given that families tend to be larger and lone parenthood is relatively more common for Aboriginal women, making that $8,000 gap very significant.

The gap between the income of Aboriginal and non-Aboriginal women, however, is much less than for their male counterparts. This reflects a number of factors including the fact women everywhere continue to assume responsibility for children that can limit their capacity to pursue education and earn income, especially when childcare and other family supports are in short supply. And gender discrimination in the labour market continues to be a fact of life for many women. While women's education attainment and labour force participation continues to increase, the gender wage gap has not improved significantly in the past two or three decades.

Census data showed that in 2000 the median family income of Aboriginal lone-mother families was $16,895 compared to $29,636 for their non-Aboriginal counterparts. Median income was highest for Métis families at $18,694, followed by Inuit families at $17,706 and First Nations families at $16,224. One-quarter (26%) of Aboriginal lone mothers reported that their incomes were less than $10,000, compared to 12% of their non-Aboriginal counterparts.[8]

QUALITY OF LIFE

Aboriginal people consistently earn less than non-Aboriginal people; as an overall trend, this gap between Aboriginal and non-Aboriginal income widened over the 20 years between 1980 and 2000, demonstrating how historical disadvantage, among other factors, has ongoing impacts on Aboriginal income.

While income is a key indicator of the quality of life that Aboriginal children and youth experience growing up, it is certainly not the only one. On almost all quality of life indicators, Aboriginal people do not fare well.

For example, Canada has always placed near the top of the United Nations Human Development Index, which ranks countries on a number of quality of life indicators, including income. According to the Assembly of First Nations' (AFN) calculations, while Canada ranked 8th in the world in 2001, First Nations communities, using the same criteria, would have ranked far lower at 76th among 174 nations.[9]

Indian and Northern Affairs Canada (INAC) also used a well-being index to examine the quality of life in 4,685 Canadian communities looking at education, labour force activity, income, and housing. Only one First Nation community came in the top 100 while 92 First Nations communities appeared in the bottom 100.[10]

POVERTY: "REAL BASIC LEVELS OF NEED"

There is no official measure of poverty in Canada, unlike in many other countries. There are several measures, however, and by any of them, Canada has a poverty problem that has been well-documented by the National Council of Welfare for over 25 years. As highlighted in our most recent report, *Poverty Profile*, poverty rates are almost exactly the same as they were 25 years ago, with the exception of seniors (see Chart 2.3). For those people who are forced to turn to welfare, our *Welfare Incomes* report

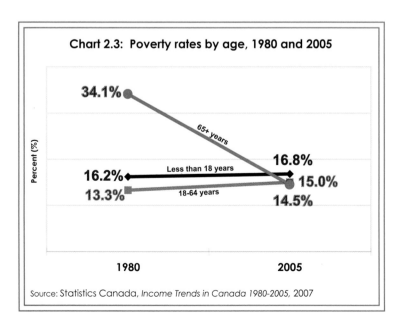

Chart 2.3: Poverty rates by age, 1980 and 2005

Source: Statistics Canada, *Income Trends in Canada 1980-2005, 2007*

showed that many welfare incomes today are lower than they were in 1986, when adjusted for inflation.

The most frequently used measure of low income in Canada is the low income cut-offs (LICOs) produced by Statistics Canada.[11] We use LICOs in this report to present data on poverty, unless otherwise indicated. However, LICOs are not available for the territories or reserves, a serious shortcoming when considering the situation of Aboriginal people in Canada.

SNAPSHOT OF ABORIGINAL POVERTY

Poverty among Aboriginal peoples tells a particular story about historical disadvantage and challenges to be overcome. The following snapshot illustrates some of the challenges.

- The 2001 Census revealed very high poverty levels:

  - Persons living in families: a poverty rate of 31% for Aboriginal people, 12% for non-Aboriginal people;

  - Persons not living in families: 56% for Aboriginal people, 38% for non-Aboriginal people;

  - Children aged 0-14: 41% for Aboriginal children, 18% for non-Aboriginal children;

  - Youth aged 15-24 living in families: 32% for Aboriginal youth, 14% for non-Aboriginal youth; and

  - Youth living independently: 75% for Aboriginal youth, 65% for non-Aboriginal youth.[12]

- In the Western provinces, a large proportion of Aboriginal children aged 0-14 lived in impoverished families: 51% in Manitoba compared to 22% for non-Aboriginal children and 52% in Saskatchewan compared to 21% for non-Aboriginal children. In Alberta, 37% of Aboriginal children lived in poverty compared to 16% of non-Aboriginal children.[13] For registered Indian children the cross Canada figure is 52% living in poverty.[14]

- Aboriginal people, in a study of 27 large metropolitan areas (CMAs), had a poverty rate of 39.4% in the year 2000.[15] This study, while indicating a decline in poverty rates from 1995, also showed that poverty rates among Aboriginal people in some city areas, such as Regina (53.2%), Saskatoon (52.5%), Winnipeg (49.1%) and Edmonton (39.1%), are two to three times the rates for non-Aboriginal people.

- In the six CMAs with large Aboriginal populations, Aboriginal people made up an increasingly larger share of the population living in poverty between 1995 and 2000 (using the low-income measure, LIM).[16]

- The 2004 Survey of Labour and Income Dynamics (SLID) showed that overall poverty rates for Aboriginal people remained about twice those of non-Aboriginal people. For Aboriginal youth aged 16-24, the percentage who were living in poverty in 2004 was 28% compared to 19% for non-Aboriginal youth. This rate was a dramatic improvement from the Aboriginal youth poverty rate of 49% in 1996.[17]

> *First Nations poverty is the single greatest social injustice facing Canada. Canada is one of the wealthiest nations, all because of the generosity and land of our ancestors. Yet First Nations endure poverty and third world conditions in their own homeland.*
>
> *This injustice is met with silence. The unacceptable is accepted.*
>
> AFN National Chief Phil Fontaine

While there is no comparable LICO data available for First Nations people living on-reserve, it is clear that poverty is a major challenge. While some reserves are economically thriving, the conditions on others have been referred to as "third-world like conditions." An assessment of First Nations communities in northwestern Ontario, based on a model used by international aid agencies, documented:

> . . . issues of desperate poverty, inadequate housing and community infrastructure, serious health and mental health concerns, barriers to economic development, family and childcare issues, needs for greater opportunities for community participation, and significant gaps in social service programs.[18]

In First Nations communities (on-reserve), the First Nations Regional Longitudinal Health Survey (RHS) found that households with children under 12 had a median household income of $19,716 in 2001. In households with both parents present, the median income was $27,385. When one parent was present, the median income was $17,737. This was far lower than the median household incomes for all Canadian families—$64,704 for two-parent families and $31,200 for lone-parent families.[19]

In the North, poverty is a day-to-day reality for too many Aboriginal families. Pauktuutit Inuit Women of Canada point out that although average income levels for Inuit people may suggest good wages, this is not a fair measure of economic well-being because the costs for goods and services in the North are extreme.[20] For example, a Statistics Canada survey from 2000/01 found that 56% of Nunavut respondents stated that they, or someone in their household, had lacked money over the past year to eat the quality or variety of food they had wanted, or had worried about not having enough to eat or had actually not had enough to eat. This was far higher than the national level of 14.7%.[21]

What poverty among Aboriginal people means on the ground, according to Peter Dinsdale, is tremendous programming needs, reliance on food banks, and cyclical poverty:

> *I'm sure your stats will reflect that half of the Aboriginal population is under*

population lives in cities today, as of 2001. And half of the Aboriginal population did not graduate from high school. We say we have a very young, a very urban, a very uneducated and a very impoverished population that we're serving. I think that has ramifications in the very essence of the kind of needs they come to us with.

We are seeing a high, high level of child poverty. Over 50% in some of the communities that we've dealt with in Ontario and we think that the national trend they are reporting is over 40% of Aboriginal children that live in urban areas live in child poverty. An astounding number, really. That manifests itself in different ways in the community centres that we have. Our workers in Friendship Centres, through a variety of programs, face challenges every day. They see babies coming in that are drinking powdered milk instead of formula. They are seeing parents who can't afford clean diapers. They are seeing families coming in for food banks as a main source of nutrition, with almost no food security.

Closely connected to Aboriginal poverty, is receipt of income or social assistance and its overwhelming inadequacy.

ABORIGINAL INCOME AND SOCIAL ASSISTANCE

The number of Aboriginal individuals and families having to rely on social or income assistance is one of Canada's great disgraces. Provincial and territorial social assistance (SA) programs are available to qualifying non-reserve Aboriginal and non-Aboriginal people while federal income assistance (IA) provided by INAC is available

on-reserve. The federal government sets on-reserve income assistance rates according to each province or territory's social assistance rates.

INAC collects data about income assistance receipt on-reserve, but there is no readily available source of comparable data about social assistance receipt by non-reserve Aboriginal people in different provinces and territories. This makes it especially difficult to understand the status and needs of Métis people and Inuit people, as well as those of First Nations people living off-reserve.

In general, it is difficult to get comparable information on social assistance. The National Council of Welfare is unique in regularly publishing information about the level of welfare incomes in its *Welfare Incomes* series. The Council hopes in the future to be able to include specific information on Aboriginal people wherever possible. Given the high rates of poverty among non-reserve Aboriginal people, their rates of dependency on social assistance are likely higher than the Canadian average. In this report on Aboriginal children and youth, data on income assistance is sourced from INAC and only includes First Nations people living on-reserve.

Income assistance beneficiaries represented 35% of on-reserve residents in 2003 compared to 5.5% of the general population receiving social assistance, as shown in Table 2.1.

Other data shows that there has been a slight decrease in the average number of monthly income assistance beneficiaries—the total number of people (children, youth and adults) receiving IA—among First Nations on-reserve, from approximately 156,629 in 1997-1998 to 149,631 in 2004-2005.[22]

Table 2.1: Comparison of Income or Social Assistance Coverage Rates— On-reserve Population and General Population, 1997 and 2003

Province/ Territory and Canada	1997			2003		
	Total Population at March, 1997	Number of People on IA or SA at March, 1997	Percentage	Total Population at March, 2003	Number of People on IA or SA at March, 2003	Percentage
General Population (excluding on-reserve population)						
Canada	29,819,070	2,774,900	9.3%	31,543,355	1,745,600	5.5%
British Columbia	3,931,016	321,300	8.1%	4,135,769	180,700	4.3%
Manitoba	1,135,851	79,100	6.9%	1,159,917	59,900	5.1%
Atlantic	2,373,558	247,300	10.4%	2,342,835	165,800	7.0%
Ontario	11,180,472	1,149,600	10.2%	12,193,256	673,900	5.5%
On-reserve Population						
Canada	369,163	152,746	41.4%	423,631	147,300	34.8%
British Columbia	72,448	22,749	31.4%	80,103	18,009	22.5%
Manitoba	62,554	29,853	47.7%	74,038	32,483	43.9%
Atlantic	15,645	12,634	80.8%	18,420	11,818	64.2%
Ontario	73,109	18,004	24.6%	82,774	18,615	22.5%

Source: INAC, *Income Assistance Reform*.

The average number of monthly IA recipients, however, has been increasing over the same period from 70,927 to 76,905.[23] "Recipient" refers to the number of families and single individuals receiving IA. The increase in recipients combined with a decrease in beneficiaries suggests that the number of dependent children has been dropping slightly. Approximately 72,000 children on-reserve live in families receiving income assistance.

Data for 2004 shows that the estimated rate of coverage for people on-reserve varies dramatically by region from 58.5% in receipt in the Atlantic region to a still outrageous low of 23% in Ontario. In the Prairies, the rates are also very high at 40.8% in Manitoba, 49.2% in Saskatchewan and 40.1% in Alberta.[24] This again illustrates that First Nations are not participating in the boom in Western Canada; Aboriginal people overwhelmingly remain on the sideline.

The majority of adult on-reserve IA recipients are young, between 18 and 40 years of age, while 60% are men and 40% are women.[25] In the general population, the majority of SA recipients tend to be older, between 40 and 64 years of age.[26]

INAC has noted,

> With the growing youth population and the number of employable youths taking up IA there is a disturbing trend emerging. The disproportionate number of youths/singles versus families taking up IA has become a generational cycle with negative implications for the communities, the youth, and the IA program.[27]

However, when there are few job or training opportunities available to Aboriginal youth, on-reserve or off, they are left with little choice. As noted by Dinsdale,

> *So, if you accept the premise that half the people that live in urban centres didn't graduate from high schools and are under the age of 25, that has a lot of programming implications. That's what we are seeing across the country. Very young people in food banks every day. As they get older, they are committing crimes of property, not crimes of passion, crimes of hunger. You know, crimes of desperation. I think that adds a unique and distinct kind of programming challenge to the work that we do. We've seen a rise in addiction levels as these people go through their lifecycles. We're seeing a very impoverished population; food security becomes an important issue. I think the unfortunate reality is that many of the programs we have focused on education are targeted at children, just post-natal up to 5. That kind of empowerment and head start programs— pre- and post-natal programs; early-parenting; and family programs, are very much focused on getting a good start.*

No Safety in the Social Safety Net

The fact that so many Aboriginal people are condemned to assistance incomes far below any poverty line is a major contributing factor to high rates of poverty for Aboriginal children and youth. The federal government has set income assistance rates on-reserve at the same rate as provincial or territorial social assistance. This means that annual rates can vary widely, for example, from $3,427 for a single person in New Brunswick to $8,198 in Newfoundland and Labrador. Provincial and territorial rates are generally low, below the poverty line.[28]

Income and social assistance policies can also be a factor in the abuse of women. The erosion of assistance rates across Canada has made it difficult for women generally to get out of and avoid abusive situations. Social assistance rates that are grossly inadequate to address the needs of women and their children can be a barrier to their ability to leave or avoid abusive relationships and assert themselves independently.

Simply put, poverty and subsistence level rates of assistance contribute to women's financial vulnerability to economic and physical abuse by leaving lower-income women without many options for survival. This dire situation for all women is further exacerbated for Aboriginal women who may have even less access to alternative housing options as discussed in the housing chapter, particularly in remote communities and on-reserve. This exposure is interconnected with other factors discussed in this report such as education, employment, wellness, and children in care.

Aboriginal children and youth are clearly impacted where a caregiver is unable to leave and remove them from an abusive situation. They may be victims of abuse themselves or may get caught up in the vicious cycle of abuse and become abusers.

It is also noteworthy that the Universal Child Care Benefit in effect as of July 1, 2006, is devised such that its benefit to Aboriginal peoples is minimized. As noted by Alistair MacPhee:

> . . . many people have not applied for the $100 a month payments. The program was initiated very quickly; so many parents did not understand that they would need to apply for the Universal Child Care Benefit. Jamie Gallant, Chief and President of the Native Council of Prince Edward Island describes the Universal Child Care Benefit as complex and confusing and lacking transparency. Many low-income Aboriginal families will end up with lower net benefits than welfare families. Lone-parent families will end up with the smallest benefits from the new program and this is unacceptable for me because of the large number of single-parent families in Aboriginal communities.

However, increases to income and social assistance rates and improvements in benefits are not a panacea for the disproportionate impoverished state of Aboriginal families, children and youth. Only a holistic, comprehensive socio economic approach can successfully tackle this oppression.

A COMPREHENSIVE APPROACH

The issue for us is that it's very hard to have a conversation about housing, and education and lifelong learning in isolation of each other as they are all part of a whole; of the whole person. We could talk about why are people not getting paid well? Why is there a poverty line? We live in poverty because we are not finishing high school. Maybe racism, that's a broader issue but leaving that aside for the moment. Maybe they aren't graduating from high school or from universities or training schools. Well why aren't they doing that? In part, because their parents never did. There's no expectations. Because of the life conditions that they live in. Why does that exist? Well that exists because of the level of disempowerment that exists in this country for generations against Aboriginal peoples. Why did that happen? If we kind of come back to a source of some of these ills, it kind of gives us as sense of how we might get out of it.

Peter Dinsdale

For Dinsdale, success in improving the lives of Aboriginal children and youth is a closely linked to Aboriginal women, collaboration, and an overarching governance approach:

I think the Royal Commission on Aboriginal People, RCAP, really sets the framework down on nation-building and maybe you should develop reconciliation, using that kind of language. I think that has its role.

It struck me last night almost a decade later, about using more the language of partnership and First Nation-driven and the First Nation example. It's important to change. One is about healing and reconciliation. The other is about acknowledging jurisdiction. I think that is an important distinction. National chiefs rightfully now argue that you need a collaborative comprehensive socioeconomic approach. If not, just deal with water. Just deal with women and children. It's sitting down with membership and leadership and saying, "Okay let's talk about what you're seeing here."

It's a recognition of your needs around your children and youth programming. Child poverty doesn't exist in isolation of family poverty. That's a reality, right? And family poverty doesn't exist just as an economic issue, but also as a social issue and you need to deal with all the social issues first before you get to the economic issues. That kind of approach is important in general.

Dinsdale notes that the Friendship Centre movement stresses the importance of holistic versus segregated approaches to education for example:

. . . none of those [segregated] measures is going to fundamentally impact the single Aboriginal women in downtown Winnipeg on

their decision about whether to drop out of school. And if we are going to be serious about addressing First Nation poverty, Inuit poverty, Canadian poverty, we have to get to that woman and her child. If that woman finishes school, she will have more money for that child to grow up in. I assure you, once she finishes school, she's going to hold on to her child, that no matter what they want to do in life they will certainly accomplish it. Success will be an option. They will work for the child and have a different standard for them and all the outcomes the rest of her family has. It breaks the cycles.

I think there also needs to be recognition that there needs to be a different approach on the ground where people's bellies are empty and they are sleeping in inadequate conditions. Whether that's outside or inside. And to attack that level of poverty and that level of issue you need to have service providers talking about how to address the need.

How do we get there? I think we get there through, again, collaborative policy processes like Kelowna with the exception that they look at the urban dilemma and they have accommodation for the service providers that ultimately have to make it happen on the ground.

And finally, Dinsdale noted the importance of Aboriginal peoples, communities and organizations working together:

I think maybe the last thing is that the Aboriginal community has a responsibility in and of ourselves, to get our relationships right. The opportunities are too few to squander them away arguing with each other over who represents who and frankly, we participated in that.

The issues we are talking about, children, youth and poverty are bigger than our organization, are bigger than our organizations, and are bigger than our egos.

It should also be noted that Aboriginal women seek greater participation and input into decision making for First Nations, Métis, and Inuit women. They seek access to the powers of Chief and Council, political participation in local and federal governance structures and participation in the negotiation and implementation of self-government agreements, legislation and policy changes. The mode of governance for Inuit peoples is, and has been, different from that imposed by the Indian Act upon First Nations; both Inuit and Métis women face distinct challenges in facilitating national dialogue on access to governance and decision making.[29]

IN SUMMARY

As an overall trend, the gap between income for Aboriginal and non-Aboriginal people across the spectrum continues to widen, demonstrating how historical disadvantage, among other factors, has ongoing impacts on the earnings of Aboriginal people.

The statistics tell a very real story of Aboriginal exclusion from economic and labour market booms, one of lack of education and opportunities, of cyclical poverty, poor health and justice outcomes and incredible numbers of Aboriginal children in care. Even during boom times, Aboriginal adults, their children and youth, remain largely on the sidelines.

The following chapters of this report examine some of these root causes and outcomes, interweaving them to tell a holistic story of Aboriginal child and youth poverty, while simultaneously profiling success stories that highlight "how we might get out of it."

CHAPTER 3

ABORIGINAL EMPLOYMENT: PICKING UP THE TOOLS

> *Poor employment outcomes are linked to high levels of economic insecurity among Aboriginal peoples, including persistent poverty, which in turn continues to profoundly influence the life chances and aspirations of Aboriginal people, their families and their communities.*
>
> Coryse Ciceri and Katherine Scott, *The Determinants of Employment Among Aboriginal Peoples*

Inequalities in the workforce clearly impact Aboriginal children and youth who depend on adults for their economic needs. Employment and unemployment patterns also have larger and longer-term impacts, affecting family relationships, self-esteem, wellness and the expectations of the next generation as children grow up. In addition, the opportunities or lack of opportunities to earn income can impact the decisions Aboriginal youth make about staying in school, as well as their very survival if they are on their own.

ABORIGINAL EMPLOYMENT: IMPROVING BUT GAPS REMAIN

Employment rates from the 2001 Census show that 49.7% of the Aboriginal population 15 years and older was employed, far below the non-Aboriginal rate of 61.8%. The First Nations on-reserve employment rate was 37.3% compared

to 54.2% for the non-reserve Aboriginal population.[1]

Aboriginal people's employment, however, is on a positive trend. Their rates increased at a faster pace than those for non-Aboriginal people from 1996-2001.[2] As indicated by Chart 3.1, over a 20-year period Aboriginal employment among

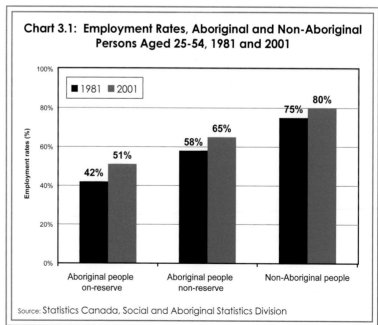

Chart 3.1: Employment Rates, Aboriginal and Non-Aboriginal Persons Aged 25-54, 1981 and 2001

Source: Statistics Canada, Social and Aboriginal Statistics Division

those in the peak earning age group of 25-54 has increased to a greater extent than for the non-Aboriginal population, but is still far behind.

One issue that affects both Aboriginal women and men is the distinction between work and employment. Raising children, hunting, fishing and other forms of economically valuable and often essential work may be done outside the cash economy. For rural and Northern populations, the allocation of time to paid and unpaid work may be quite different than in large, urban centres, for example.

Factors such as family size and the availability of childcare, training or transportation can affect individual ability to take advantage of employment opportunities. In addition, better-off Canadians often do not understand how much work goes into surviving on incomes that are a fraction of the poverty line. The lack of paid job opportunities and community economic development strategies in some communities are also factors that act as barriers to finding and keeping a job.

ABORIGINAL UNEMPLOYMENT: GREATER THAN FOR OTHER CANADIANS

Not only are Aboriginal people less likely to have a paid job, they are more likely to be looking for one. In 2001, the unemployment rate for Aboriginal people 15 years and older was 19.1%, compared to non-Aboriginal Canadians at 7.1%.[3] Unemployed people are those who are not working for pay or profit, but who are looking for such work.

On-reserve, the unemployment situation for First Nations is far worse. In 2001, the unemployment rate for First Nations people living on-reserve was 27.8% compared to 16.5% for the non-reserve Aboriginal population.[4] However, Indian and Northern Affairs Canada observed that the unemployment rate on some reserves can reach as high as 70% or more.[5]

In Manitoba and Saskatchewan, unemployment rates were over three times as high for Aboriginal people compared to those for non-Aboriginal people in 2001. Relative rates are a little better in the other provinces and territories, but still range from 1.5 to 2.9 times as high.[6]

This pattern of inequality is evident even for Aboriginal people aged 25-54 with post-secondary degrees who had higher unemployment rates than non-Aboriginal people with similar education. The 2001 Census showed that the highest unemployment rates in this group were for status Indians and Inuit, though all Aboriginal people suffered higher unemployment rates.[7]

GENDER COUNTS

In the overall population, increases in employment in recent decades have to a great extent been the result of a growth in women's employment, especially women with children. Aboriginal women are less likely to be employed than Aboriginal men or non-Aboriginal women, however, and this pattern is related to gender, demographic and historical factors.

Traditional gender divisions of labour have an impact; women remain most often the primary caregivers of children. Aboriginal women have more children on average, have them at an earlier age and are more likely to be lone-parents, all of which affects their labour market situation, particularly given the lack of quality childcare almost everywhere in Canada.

Aboriginal women experience lower incomes than Aboriginal men or other women.[8] Lone parents are less likely to be employed than persons living alone or married; and the presence of young children has a great impact on the likelihood of the lone parent's employment.[9]

In his study of Aboriginal lone mothers in Canada, Hull concluded:

> All Canadian single mothers tend to experience economic disadvantages, including problems in the labour market and low family income, but Aboriginal single mothers experience these problems to a greater degree than others. The low incomes of single mother families and high rates of dependency on government transfer payments among Aboriginal single mothers are clearly documented.[10]

The situation for young Aboriginal women is the worst, given not only high rates of lone parenthood in the Aboriginal community but also high rates of teenage parenthood.

In the Western provinces in 2006, young Aboriginal men aged 15-24 (who were not students and not living on a reserve) had an unemployment rate of 14.2% compared to 7.9% for non-Aboriginal young men. Their female counterparts fared even less well with an unemployment rate of 16.9% compared to 6.3% for non-Aboriginal young women.[11]

Higher unemployment rates combined with lower wages for Aboriginal women and youth often translate into lives of poverty for their children.

BIG GAPS EQUAL BIG IMPLICATIONS

Studies have indicated that educational attainment is a key determinant of employment for Aboriginal people.[12] In fact, recent research by Ciceri and Scott indicates that the rate of return for higher levels of education is greater for Aboriginal people.[13]

Other factors influencing lower employment rates and higher unemployment rates for Aboriginal people include elevated migration rates for the population. Migration within the last year has been linked to decreased odds of employment.[14]

The health status of workers is also an influential factor in employment as are disability rates; once again disproportionately high in the Aboriginal population.[15]

Systemic racism clearly also plays a role, for example as a factor in the higher unemployment rates for Aboriginal people with a post-secondary education compared to non-Aboriginal people.

While the contributing factors are many and interconnected, poor employment rates for Aboriginal people have very clear implications.

As indicated by Garry Jobin, chronic unemployment within families has a cyclical effect on youth:

You've got to be an older brother to a lot of these kids because many of them never saw their parents go to work. They don't understand when they are going to be late for work, they have to call, and when they miss a day they have to call. And when they are getting their paycheques and going out and partying and not making it to work, losing jobs, you've got to be there to kind of hold on to them.

A lot of our young people who are in Blade Runners are 19, 20 years old with two kids at home with a 17 year old wife. So, you're mentoring them and teaching them how to be a parent, responsible, how to budget money, helping them set up bank accounts, trying to reconnect them with their families, and just being a shoulder for them to lean on.

Given the responsibilities faced by many Aboriginal youth coupled with their burgeoning population, the employment opportunities available to them are relevant to the economies and well-being of both Aboriginal and mainstream communities.

ABORIGINAL YOUTH FACE GREATER CHALLENGES

Within the youth age group, usually considered to be 15 to 24, there may be students living at home who may or may not be employed as well as graduates and school leavers living on their own or even raising families.

In 2000, among Aboriginal youth who were employed, 17% worked full-time, full-year and 83% worked part-time, similar to the breakdown for non-Aboriginal youth.[16]

However, unemployment rates tell the story of youth who want and need a job but do not have one. Unemployment rates for Aboriginal youth were roughly double those for non-Aboriginal youth in 2001. For on-reserve First Nations youth, the unemployment rate was 40.8% compared to 23% for non-reserve Aboriginal youth and 13.2% for all non-Aboriginal youth.[17]

Dr. Cathy Richardson, speaking about the importance of gainful employment for Métis youth, observed,

Part of the problem I think for young people, for adolescents, is that generally in society they are not seen as having very much value. They are not seen as contributing. They are often perceived as being sluggish or dangerous. Particularly if for various reasons they leave school.

Okalik Eegeesiak commented on the employment opportunities, or lack thereof, for Inuit youth:

Without the proper education, it's minimal. I mean, with some of the unemployment rates that we have in the communities it is 90%. How do we get from 90% unemployment to 7% which is the national unemployment rate?

And in the North, says Eegeesiak, not all youth can move to find employment,

There's lots of people in Iqaluit from other communities because the jobs are in Iqaluit. The types of job they are interested in are in Iqaluit. People move where there's opportunities, but

then some people don't, as well. And because there are no jobs in the communities, they don't work.

And while the Nunavut government has programs integrating Inuit youth into government jobs says Eegeesiak,

> *. . . the intent is there. But the kids aren't educated. They don't have enough education or experience. I think the intent of government is there to increase Inuit employment.*

Commenting on the greatest barriers to Aboriginal youth employment today, Jobin says,

> *. . . youth are facing a lot of barriers out there: to employment, housing, the legal system, welfare system, and having a young family; housing is probably the biggest crisis facing our kids.*

> *It's just somebody believing in them and somebody there to hold their hand until they are ready to stand on their own two feet. I do strongly believe we have the people with the experience, the skills, and the passion that can be successful in anything they want to do.*

Blade Runners is an award winning employment program assisting multi-barrier and disadvantaged youth in gaining on-the-job construction training and apprenticeships. Registered Indian youth make up 95% of Blade Runners participants, all are aged 15-30 and 25% are female. They have multiple barriers to employment, says Jobin,

> *. . . they grew up in the foster care system, grew up in the cycle of income assistance, were involved in substance abuse issues, doing B & Es (break and enters). And a lot of them ran away because there was not much support*

at home and ended up on the streets of the downtown Eastside, downtown Granville or Commercial Drive. A lot of them don't have the best education in the world because mainstream school just did not work out for them. I mean you're going to school and you haven't got a lunch, you have no school supplies, and what do you think you are going to be thinking about. . . getting the next meal.

> *We have an 80% success rate of kids that go to a construction site and 2 years later are working in the construction trade. In those 2 years they may have lost 3 or 4 jobs, but what you did was you turned a different light bulb on in their head to say yeah I don't want that life anymore.*

Many of the Blade Runners are short on the education they need to succeed:

> *. . . We know in an interview that they have to go back to school by how they fill out an application, but we don't tell them that, we feed them the candy first. Let them go out there and get the experience first. We do a three month performance evaluation after a long-term attachment to the work place. If the evaluation goes great, then we have to talk to him about going back to school and taking a math class once or twice a week in an outreach program in the downtown eastside or the native education centre. So, encouraging them to go back to school is a part of the job as well.*

The Aboriginal population has the youth and the ability to fill the gaps in the work force as the mainstream population continues to age, particularly in those areas of the country with a booming economy.

THE CASE OF WESTERN CANADA:
GOOD ECONOMIC CONDITIONS ARE NOT ENOUGH

Some important additional detail about Aboriginal people in the workforce is located in the Labour Force Survey[18] for the four western provinces, although it does not include on-reserve data. This survey highlights some recent trends in the labour force for Aboriginal people, including youth. The data for 2004, 2005 and the first nine months of 2006 are particularly of interest, given that this is a generally favourable economic period for the west and a boom period for Alberta. The results provide an indication of the limited degree to which Aboriginal peoples are sharing the benefits of a positive economic environment.

ABORIGINAL UNEMPLOYMENT REMAINS HIGH

Even for Aboriginal people with higher education in a high growth economy, the risk of unemployment is great. In 2006, Aboriginal people aged 15-64 with a university education had an unemployment rate double that of similarly educated non-Aboriginal people. Aboriginal youth aged 15-24 who completed post-secondary education experienced unemployment rates more than double the rate of their non-Aboriginal counterparts.

For Aboriginal youth not in school, the unemployment rate was 15.4%, more than double the 7.2% for non-Aboriginal youth. For First Nations youth, the percentage jumps to 21.7% or three times the rate for non-Aboriginal youth. Métis workers were better-off at 11% but still experienced greater unemployment than the non-Aboriginal group. When students are included, the overall unemployment rates for youth show similar trends.

As Chart 3.2 indicates, in each of the four provinces in western Canada unemployment rates for Aboriginal youth were far higher than those of non-Aboriginal youth.

In the booming Alberta economy, the 2006 Aboriginal youth unemployment rate was 12%, almost double the 6.4% rate for non-Aboriginal youth. For First Nations, the unemployment rate was even higher at 15.6%.

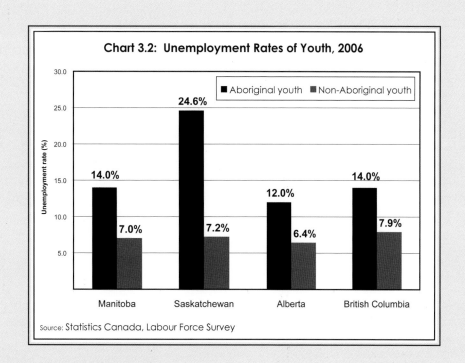

Chart 3.2: Unemployment Rates of Youth, 2006

Source: Statistics Canada, Labour Force Survey

EMPLOYMENT GROWTH: ABORIGINAL PEOPLE NOT RECEIVING FULL BENEFIT

When we look at employment and job growth trends, it is clear that Aboriginal workers are not yet full participants in the western economic boom. The number of Aboriginal people who were employed increased 10% between 2004 and 2006, a considerable improvement, but their employment rates still trail those of non-Aboriginal people. By 2006, 66.1% of non-Aboriginal people were employed in western Canada compared to 60.9% of Aboriginal people.

There are significant differences, however, by employment sector and by Aboriginal groups. Métis young people, in particular, emerged as a growing labour force between 2004 and 2006, expanding by over 4,000 employed while First Nations numbers were stagnant.

Overall gains have been made in the service, construction and healthcare sector in Aboriginal employment, but less so in the overall goods sector, public administration or accommodation and food services. In Alberta, for example. Aboriginal youth have gained some 2,300 jobs in the generally lower paying service sector where they now total 16,600 employed.

In the mining, oil and gas industries, all boom industries in western Canada, employment has not been booming among Aboriginal workers. While total new jobs in this sector for all ages grew by almost 30,000 in three years from 145,200 to 176,900, the numbers of Aboriginal workers in this sector actually declined to 5,600 from 6,300 in 2004.

There has been some growth in the mining, oil and gas sector for Aboriginal workers aged 15-29, however, including a 33% increase from 1,200 to 1,600 employed in Alberta. The non-Aboriginal group in Alberta grew from 29,300 to 38,400, a 31% increase. The 1,600 Aboriginal workers made up 4% of the total workers in this sector, while Aboriginal workers 15-29 made up 5% of the workforce.

WAGES STILL LOWER

Wages remain much lower for Aboriginal employees than for non-Aboriginal employees. For example, the average weekly wage in the western provinces for non-Aboriginal people is $759 and for Aboriginal people it is $614 or 81%. For First Nations it is even less at 78% of the non-Aboriginal wage.

For First Nations men the difference in wages is about $220 per week, giving them about 75% of non-Aboriginal wages. For women the difference is less at $93 per week or 85% of non-Aboriginal women's wages, an indicator of the low value of women's wages in general compared to men's. Even Aboriginal people with a university degree earn only 78% of non-Aboriginal wages.

Numerous studies over the years have identified a myriad of interconnected reasons for these poor wage outcomes, including low levels of educational attainment; a comparatively young population; the geographical location of many Aboriginal peoples; lack of training and of language proficiency; gender; and not least, discrimination in the labour market.[19]

The overall rate of unionization of Aboriginal people in western Canada, at 29.9% of those employed, is not much different from the non-Aboriginal rate of 30.7%. However, the rate for First Nations is still lower at 26.2%, while that for Métis is 32.8%. This factor can help explain some of the wage differentials between Métis and First Nations; however, both groups have average wages below those of non-Aboriginal people.

UNDERSTANDING THE INEQUALITIES

As noted by Peter Dinsdale:

> That's intriguing because they are flying people in from Newfoundland and from all over across the ocean they come and fill these jobs. We brief MPs on a variety of issues and the MPs responsible for the Fort McMurray ridings and around talk about the fact that Tim Horton's is paying $16 an hour for dish washers. Many non-profits, not just the Friendship Centre, are having problems staffing because why would you be a program director at the Centre for $18 an hour if you can get the same being a waiter? It's less stress on you and you get tips.

> So it is shocking that given the employment boom and resources that could exist if we educated them right and trained them right that more partnerships and more development is not occurring. Is it racism? Is it lack of connection? I'm not really sure what the issue is. Some are successful in industries and great for them. It's a peculiar employment puzzle—we should follow up more on why that is.

Dr. Richardson commented on the quality of Aboriginal employment available,

> Again, the globalization trend has meant that many of the jobs in Victoria are in the service industry and we have lowered the minimum wage here over the past 6-8 years and there seems to be more and more pressure on workers. The government tends to support business or small business people so it's really hard to find a decent job and make a good living and be proud of what you do. I think if people can't find work then they are often kept apart from any kind of dignity or having a chance of a decent lifestyle or looking after their children properly.

> I know that there are lots of Métis people, too, who do very dangerous jobs. If you look at Fort McMurray and that kind of mining and oil-related work—there's lots of Métis people there.

PARTNERING FOR SUCCESS

Canada is experiencing a demographic slowdown in population replacement while the Aboriginal population is growing at a rapid rate. Improving access to the labour market for Aboriginal people is first and foremost about addressing centuries of inequality. It is also about meeting Canada's labour market needs as the mainstream workforce continues to age.

The challenges are succinctly stated by Ciceri and Scott:

> The problem is unsupportive learning environments. The problem is the health and sustainability of Aboriginal communities. The problem is the historic legacy of colonialism and racism. Part of the answer strongly suggested by our study is the critical need to increase the educational attainment of Aboriginal people.
>
> Resources are also needed to encourage Aboriginal people to pursue post-secondary training, and to support other working-age adults via continuing education and skills upgrading, literacy and basic skills development, apprenticeships and employment training, and job preparation and mentoring—with programs that are both culturally sensitive and inclusive. At the same time, investment in childcare, transportation, assistance with other work-related expenses, as well as secure housing, is a prerequisite for any successful initiative.[20]

Ciceri and Scott stress the need for a holistic approach, one that focuses not only on skills preparation or job readiness, but also incorporates the family, the community and the roles of women, among other factors.

That's where success stories like Blade Runners come in. The Blade Runners program has met with tremendous success, explains Jobin, but could do more with greater support from the business community, industry, and all governments.

It is after all, Jobin adds,

> . . . an economic windfall as well because your tax paying dollars aren't going to keep them on the cycle of income assistance, you're not paying for incarcerations, you're not paying for court costs, and more importantly you're not paying to bury the young person because they have lost hope and given up on society. They are spending their paycheques in the community, and for a lot of our young Blade Runners their kids at home are seeing mommy or daddy go out to work everyday.

He believes we can turn it around: *"stay with the people, believe in the people, and give them an opportunity and they will thrive."*

While most segments of Canada's population are ageing rapidly, Canada's younger Aboriginal population is able to meet many labour market needs as well as their own, given opportunities in education, training and access.

We have the tools; we need only pick them up.

IN SUMMARY

Despite the disadvantage Aboriginal peoples have experienced in the labour force to date, the youthfulness of the population renders Aboriginal peoples well positioned to move into the workforce en masse as the overall population continues to age. Such a transition would be of benefit to both Aboriginal and non-Aboriginal communities and economies.

Transformation of dismal unemployment rates and the lack of employment opportunities for Aboriginal peoples requires:

- a holistic approach to the reasons why they have been marginalized in the first place;

- an emphasis on educational attainment and family supports; and

- an expansion of program approaches that are shown to be working.

Such an approach should focus not only on jobs, but also on the family and the community with a particular emphasis on the role of women.

Existing inequalities in the workforce continue to impact Aboriginal children and youth whether as dependants or participants in the workforce; simultaneously, current economic and demographic conditions provide a unique opportunity to open doors to employment.

CHAPTER 4

ABORIGINAL CHILDREN AND YOUTH: EDUCATION, LANGUAGE AND CULTURE

Most of my teachers were all right, except for my math teacher... he was... racist against three Natives in the class... me and two of my friends. On the first days we got to class, he put us in a different room and said you guys can work on this because I don't think you can keep up with what we're doing in the classroom... We all did our work just to prove to him that, if you say we're that dumb... well we're not... We didn't say anything about it, but what could you do?

Quote from Laura Metcalfe, *Exploring Empowering Education for Marginalized Youth in Toronto*

First Nations, Métis and Inuit children and youth are not receiving an education equivalent to that of other Canadian children and youth, regardless of where they live. From pre-school and early learning through to post-secondary education (PSE), Aboriginal peoples are receiving less education than non-Aboriginal Canadians and are facing more and greater barriers. Nor are their Aboriginal languages and cultures being adequately transmitted and preserved, either through the education system or otherwise.

EARLY LEARNING AND CHILDCARE

Public spending on early childhood education and care in countries similar to Canada ranges from 0.4% to 2% of the gross domestic product (GDP). According to the Organization for Economic Co-operation and Development,

Canada ranks at the bottom, with 0.2% of GDP in this area of spending.[1]

This general under-investment in early learning has serious consequences for Aboriginal children. For example, there are 257 First Nations communities without access to childcare and many more communities do not have enough spaces to support even 20% of children from birth to six years of age.[2]

As stated by the Congress of Aboriginal Peoples (CAP):

> Little is known about the health and development of young Aboriginal children in Canada. In particular, comprehensive national data concerning Aboriginal children off-reserve is not readily available—especially for children 0-5.[3]

According to Alastair MacPhee:

> *Aboriginal children face a far greater risk than non-Aboriginal children and because of this vulnerability, it places special emphasis on*

the need for Aboriginal childcare and an early learning initiative that includes all Aboriginal children regardless of residence.

Childcare and early learning programs need to be culturally sensitive to Aboriginal people. Social service programs for Aboriginal children off-reserve (status and non-status Indians) and Métis need to be strengthened.

For Inuit children, there are about 1,500 childcare spaces provided through the First Nations and Inuit Child Care Initiative and the Aboriginal Head Start Initiative.[4] But this is far from meeting the need.

As observed by Okalik Eegeesiak, the limited number of spaces for Inuit are *"because we don't have the infrastructure for the daycare."*

As noted in the Demographics Chapter, far more Aboriginal children live in lone-parent families where the need for early childhood educational access and childcare is all the more crucial.

PROGRAM DEVELOPMENT

Some of the Aboriginal children's programs in place across the country include:

- The First Nations and Inuit Child Care Initiative provides 7,500 subsidized childcare spaces at some 407 sites in First Nation and Inuit communities;

- The Government of Canada together with the Government of Alberta funded 762 First Nations childcare spaces available to children under age 12 in 15 reserve communities in 2003–2004;

- The Government of Canada with the Government of Ontario provided

childcare services to 2,797 children under age six at 57 sites in 51 First Nations communities in 2003–2004.[5]

One major federal program, Aboriginal Head Start, comprises a series of programs but most often consists of half days, five days a week, for children aged 3–5. Aboriginal Head Start is a Health Canada-funded, early intervention strategy for First Nations, Inuit and Métis children and their families living in urban centres, large northern communities and on-reserve. The program has six components: education and school readiness; Aboriginal culture and language; parental involvement; health promotion; nutrition; and social support.

In 2003, Aboriginal Head Start in Urban and Northern Communities provided services to 3,616 children. In 2003–2004, Aboriginal Head Start On-Reserve provided services to 9,101 children at 354 project sites serving 383 communities.[6]

Aboriginal Head Start is regarded by many as one of the best programs around. Dr. Valerie Gideon notes, for example, that First Nations children who have attended are *"close to 40% less likely to repeat a grade."* Aboriginal Head Start, however, serves only some 12% of eligible children on-reserve and 7.6% living elsewhere.[7] While this program is considered positive, it is very limited in terms of reach.

As noted by MacPhee,

> *Over the past thirty-six years, a public policy struggle has taken place for a national child care program that is inclusive of Aboriginal childcare services. This struggle has involved interjurisdictional wrangling that is very familiar to status and non-status*

Indians living of-reserve and Métis. The need for Aboriginal childcare services has been advocated by CAP for many years. In 1989, we called for a federal childcare policy based on the principles of accessibility, affordability and quality, and managed by Aboriginal peoples. In 2005, we supported the QUAD principles (Quality, Universally Inclusive, Accessible and Developmental) to ensure that all Aboriginal children, regardless of residence, have the very best start in life by receiving the best possible stimulation and nourishment.

MacPhee stresses that "*early learning and childcare initiatives must incorporate a disability lens to assess and address the impact of all policies, programs and decisions on Aboriginal children with disabilities.*"

The development of Aboriginal early learning and childcare programs must also incorporate an analysis of history and the role of major institutions in the lives of Aboriginal peoples that explain their marginal position in Canadian society.[8]

KINDERGARTEN TO SECONDARY SCHOOL

Once Aboriginal children are in the formal school system there is a shortage of programming options to facilitate their learning and keep them in school and out of trouble.

Peter Dinsdale explains the educational/ recreational void for Aboriginal children:

There's a tremendous programming gap from that mythical 5-year old, 6 year-old age group where they are supposed to be going to Grade 1 through to some kind of teen

program for recreation. . . but there's almost no programming in urban areas across the country distinctly targeted at Aboriginal people.

I understand the Government of Ontario just released a pilot project for that population, ages 6-12, through Friendship Centres. That's a tremendous success. That's really best practices.

Friendship Centres try to have a cradle-to-grave mentality in terms of programming—that if you have a need in that spectrum, there would be something there for you. For early children again we do have some nutrition, parenting programs, family programs. Six to twelve is a very tough population to serve…we need a comprehensive physical activity and recreation program really to be able to do some targeted interventions for that age group.

David Budd observes that getting children into an after school program can be relatively simple:

. . . one of the things we do is offer snacks. Because some of them live in poverty, food is high priority. Outings, they like to go out. They're always in their own neighborhood, they don't get to go out.

Aboriginal education needs to be viewed on a continuum, such that secondary school non-completion rates are addressed not only at that level, but also through early learning, elementary school and external programs. Prevention is a holistic principle; in the education context it means addressing the reasons why Aboriginal students drop out before completing secondary school, or "age out" and do not return.

SECONDARY SCHOOL

Clearly, there are unique reasons underlying disproportionate Aboriginal rates of non-completion of secondary school. In the overall Canadian population in 2001, 31% had not graduated from high school, compared to 48% of Aboriginal people. Forty-two percent of Métis, 51% of the First Nation population and 58% of Inuit had not graduated from high school.[9]

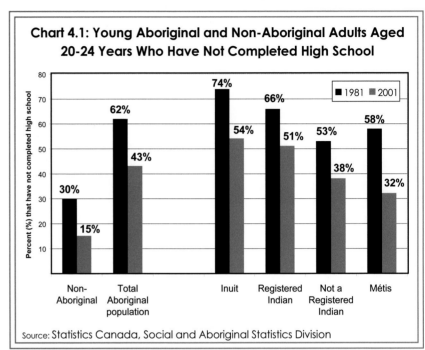

Chart 4.1: Young Aboriginal and Non-Aboriginal Adults Aged 20-24 Years Who Have Not Completed High School

Source: Statistics Canada, Social and Aboriginal Statistics Division

This is an overall gap of 17 percentage points. This gap varies across Canada, from a high of 20 points in Quebec and the Northwest Territories to a low of one point in Newfoundland and Labrador.[10] However, the lowest gap in Newfoundland does not arise because Aboriginal people have high secondary school completion rates but rather because the province has overall above average rates of non-completion.

In 2001, 15% of all Canadians aged 20–24 did not have a high school certificate compared to 43% of Aboriginal youth that age. Figures for different groups range from 54% for Inuit to 32% for Métis, as indicated in Chart 4.1. As high and disproportionate as these numbers are, they indicate a vast improvement in Aboriginal secondary school completion rates between 1981 and 2001.

As discussed in the section below on post-secondary education, this success has much to do with Aboriginal communities taking some control and direction over education. Aboriginal peoples have been striving to become more educated, and community control of Aboriginal education has rendered that goal more accessible.

However, despite this improvement for Aboriginal peoples, the gap with non-Aboriginal people remains sizable.

On-reserve, the figures for non-completion are most dismal; as noted by the AFN: "Currently only 32% of First Nation children are graduating from Grade 12-13 in on-reserve schools. This statistic has been consistent since 1994 and into 2000. That is, 70% of our population has less than a high school education." [11]

PUSH AND PULL FACTORS

Maria Wilson observed:

> I would say the main issues that children and Inuit youth face are the same issues that their parents are facing at the moment. I would say for Inuit youth, out of 100 high school students, only 25 graduate or finish high school. It is a very, very bad number. It all comes down to financial problems, infrastructure and housing problems and poverty.
>
> Education plays a huge role. They are unable to fill the workforce in Nunavut with Inuit employees because people lack necessary skills and education levels. Why? Because of multiple social and economic problems.

For example, Wilson continues:

> For a young person, even if that young person goes to high school, but then there is a job available that does not require say a high school diploma or anything and it pays up to $20 an hour or more that person would certainly drop school and go work because he or she can support himself and support the family. The irrelevance of school curriculum to traditional Inuit knowledge and culture also plays a role; many young people are troubled because of the confusion in cultural identity: how does one act in this world, as an Inuk or as Qallunaat? The situation is also aggravated by lack of early career counselling, strong community and parental engagement.

Related to the socioeconomic problems is the weight of history, says Dinsdale:

> The other qualifier I might say is that we need to look seriously at the kind of education support we provide that 12 and over age group. We know many of our people aren't graduating high school and they are dropping out after grade 8 or 9. These are the transition years when the weight of their family history and their nation's history begins to weigh them down along with the issues they're facing in communities. It's easier with no culture of achievement in education and families to simply move on and do whatever their family has done.

Budd recalls experiencing the dropout rates for Aboriginal youth first hand in an educational system that wasn't culturally appropriate:

> It just happened to me too; I lost a lot of class mates around the time of 14 or so. Grade 7 to 9 they dropped out like flies. I am thinking back how they lost interest. School became boring, they said: It's mundane. We have been doing this for how many years and are still carrying on reading and writing and all that. It does not have a sense of reflecting balance. I think about the medicine wheel. We divide the medicine wheel into quadrants and talk about the emotional and mental aspects. That is a whole approach to life.
>
> In the European system you are just half a human being. They were not interested in my spirit and not interested in my emotion. Not once did the teacher ask me how I was feeling. But they make sure I'm always learning and had gym time. They looked after those two quadrants. I think to keep the interest levels of the youth in school that's the challenge right there.

Dinsdale stresses the importance of keeping Aboriginal youth in secondary school:

> We know that's the target age group; we know what the issues are. There are some examples of successful programming out there that target

that very population. In eight Friendship Centres in Ontario, and one in B.C. and elsewhere we have alternative schools in Friendship Centres targeted to that population. Kids that have dropped out of high school are able to go back and get reintegrated back into the education system in the Friendship Centres that they go to already. They access all the other cultural and health and human services that are available at the Friendship Centre to provide a blanket of services around that child. To help them finish school. The same curriculum. The same rigorous standards and a shot in a fair and appropriate manner. Expansion of that program to other areas is wholly appropriate for that population.

Dinsdale is optimistic about programming with the ability to make a difference in Aboriginal youth graduation from secondary school:

Let me say quickly, if we have a Friendship Centre that has its gym open on a Friday night to play basketball or floor hockey, volleyball, whatever they're interested in, pow wow dancing, whatever they're interested in, kids that are taking part in that are way less likely to be out drinking or breaking into places, making babies or doing any other kinds of activities that we are trying to address. They could be accessing positive programs, could be doing so, so much. Getting them back to school to finish. It's an incredibly important population to target, again having tremendous justice outcomes.

There are additional reasons for optimism. Aboriginal high school completion rates are much higher in the 25-44 age group than in the 15-24 range due to high rates of continuing education. For example, registered status Indians aged 15-24 have a rate of 50.3% secondary school completion while those 25-44 have a rate of 69.9%.[12]

It is also very important to note that Aboriginal women are more likely than non-Aboriginal women or Aboriginal and non-Aboriginal men to return to school in later life.[13]

This indicates that while many Aboriginal people may drop out of high school, there is a strong desire for education; removal of barriers would see secondary school educational outcomes for youth and adults improve.

Budd suggests that Aboriginal youth need to be more involved in their educational choices, which must also be culturally appropriate:

Has an evaluation ever been handed out to them? They have a voice too. What are we missing, how can the school make you welcome to keep you guys here?

We have to calm them down and talk to them and ask: "what do you need my boy and my girl?" with kindness that the old people always talked about, to listen to them. I talk about that medicine wheel to get that balance in their life.

Maybe we should take them out to the bush a little bit or something like that or some other aspect of our culture.

In a National Aboriginal Health Organization survey, Aboriginal youth asked about the greatest issues facing them identified education, racism and gangs as the leading general youth issues/priorities.[14]

Further, Aboriginal youth who participated in an education study in Toronto noted racism in the education system in urban areas as a major challenge and disincentive to continuing their education.

One young Aboriginal woman described the racist way in which her non-Aboriginal friends spoke to her:

> I'll get jokes from my friends and they'd be like 'hey, squaw', or whatever, but it doesn't bother me. . . you know how some Indians are like alcoholics, they'd be like, 'yo, did you drink any listerine today?' I was like, 'no'. . . but I think, what if they actually think I do. . .[15]

Some of the participants drew links between being the targets of racism and leaving or wanting to leave school, as noted by one young Aboriginal woman: "They can't handle the stress of being alone. . . of carrying just being Native, like the only one, it's hard standing up. . . It's a stereotype that all Natives are no good. . . They hear this constantly, then they'll say, 'Yeah, they're gonna say that, even if I'm not doing it. Well fine. . . I'll do it.' "[16]

This experience of systemic racism and alienation in secondary education can be referred to as the "push factor" in that it may push Aboriginal students out of school; financial needs and the lure of employment may be referred to as the "pull factor."[17] A holistic response to Aboriginal non-completion rates requires addressing both push and pull factors.

POST-SECONDARY EDUCATION

It is regarding university graduates that the gap between Aboriginal and non-Aboriginal is the widest. Fifteen percent of non-Aboriginal Canadians over 25 had a university degree in 2001, roughly double the 8% of Aboriginal people.[18]

The gap varies across Canada with British Columbia, Ontario and the Yukon showing a 12 percentage point gap compared to Newfoundland and Labrador at five points with respect to university completion rates for the Aboriginal and non-Aboriginal population.[19]

Twenty-one percent of Inuit, 23% of the First Nation population and 29% of Métis have a post-secondary certificate/degree/diploma.[20] The 16% of Aboriginal people 25 years of age and over who possess a trade certificate is three percentage points higher than the 13% of non-Aboriginal people who also possess a trade certificate.[21] With respect to college diplomas, 18% of non-Aboriginal people over 25 possess one, only slightly higher than the 15% of Aboriginal people.[22]

From 1996-2001, the proportion of Aboriginal people aged 25 to 64 with some post-secondary qualifications (trades, college and university certification combined) increased from 33% to 38%.[23]

Only 10% of Aboriginal men have some university education compared to 14% of Aboriginal women.[24] Nine percent of Aboriginal women compared to 16% of Aboriginal men had trades certification in 2001. Seven percent of Aboriginal men and 12% of Aboriginal women had other non-university certificates.[25]

SUCCESS STORIES

In a recent speech, Phil Fontaine, National Chief of the AFN noted the success First Nations have recently been achieving in the educational realm:

> In the space of 50 years, there were 10 First Nations students in university in all of Canada, 10 in 1952. Today there are close to 30,000.

> That should tell Canadians and of course we understand this, that investing in our young people's future through education represents a significant return on the investment. And the reason we were able, or the reason we've been able to achieve such success is because government finally came to understand that our people have to own education in our communities. Control has to be exercised by our people over the education system in our communities.

> That's when the turnaround occurred. Until then we'd experienced failure. And this only happened in 1972. In 1973 it was when First Nation communities moved to exercise local control over education. And so what has that brought our community and Canada? All kinds of outstanding people in every discipline that exists out there. Outstanding doctors, lawyers, judges, social workers, pharmacists.[26]

Importantly, research has also established that post-secondary education (PSE) in the First Nations community has an intergenerational effect:

> One of the brightest rays of hope lies in the finding that there are community correlates with educational achievement. The most promising is that as the average level of education increases in the parental population, there are incremental gains in students' level of achievement.[27]

There are other success stories in Aboriginal post-secondary education programming. Wilson cites Nunavut Sivuniksavut as a very successful program:

> *The success is, let's say, of 100 students who have graduated from the program, about 80 of them find jobs in the Government of Nunavut, federal government departments, non-govermental organizations or private companies.*

This is a two-year program that prepares Nunavut students to transition from high school to college or university. Approximately 20 students a year are accepted. They go through the process of living in an urban setting with support while taking a preparatory program in Ottawa affiliated with Algonquin College.

Success, however, does not come easily as barriers persist.

SYSTEMIC RACISM AND OTHER BARRIERS

One educator who participated in a Toronto study described his own frustrations as an Aboriginal student, feeling that he was solely responsible for challenging racism:

> I had to argue with professors. . . be the spokesman for all Native people all over the world. Those are big obstacles, and they're very tiring, and exhausting. There was a time where I felt, I don't need this and I'm going to go somewhere I don't have to put up with this, with ignorance. . . with racists.[28]

Lack of resources is also consistently cited as a reason why Aboriginal people do not obtain post-secondary education. Factors related to financial causes were frequently given as reasons for non-completion of post-secondary education.

However, while 24% of men listed financial reasons, 34% of women aged 25-44 noted family responsibilities.[29] Given that Aboriginal women tend to have more children, have children at a younger age and to be lone parents, the resources they require include childcare and other family-related supports, in addition to financing for their studies.

A recent study by the Millennium Scholarship Fund analysed the barriers to post-secondary education, finding that:

> Among First Nations youth not planning to go on to college or university, financial barriers are most frequently cited as holding them back: 59% say they have to work to support their family while 40% say they do not have enough money. . . When those youth who are planning to go to post-secondary education are asked if anything might change their plans, 48% say it would be a lack of money, 43% say they may need to work to support their family and 42% say it would be because their grades are not good enough.[30]

The AFN notes,

> There is an urgent need to address the backlog of First Nations students who wish to attend PSE programs but cannot, due to the lack of adequate funding. It is estimated that approximately 10,000 First Nations PSE applicants were unable to access funding.[31]

Post-secondary education support is provided by INAC to status Indians and Inuit. Off-reserve status Indians must apply to their bands for funding which may not always be available.

Inuit frequently face additional challenges in obtaining post-secondary education related to location; Eegeesiak notes that most Inuit who want to go to university or college have to come south. This requires leaving the traditional support systems and facing a very different cultural environment that can be alienating, along with exposure to racial discrimination.

The majority of Aboriginal people—non-status Indians and Métis—do not have access to INAC funding for post-secondary education. They must apply for provincial and Canada student loans and assume the high-debt burden this entails. This can be riskier and more expensive for Aboriginal students given that degree holders still have lower incomes than non-Aboriginal degree holders, as shown in Chart 4.2:

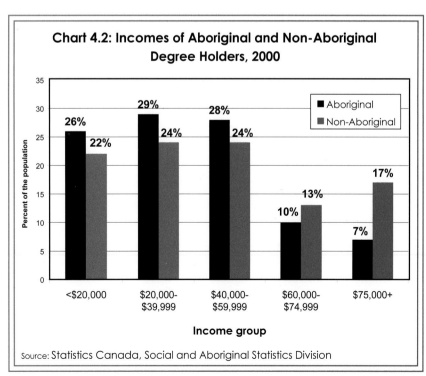

Chart 4.2: Incomes of Aboriginal and Non-Aboriginal Degree Holders, 2000

Source: Statistics Canada, Social and Aboriginal Statistics Division

ABORIGINAL LANGUAGES AND CULTURES

LANGUAGE EROSION

The 2001 Census shows a decline in the number of Aboriginal mother tongue speakers from 208,600 in 1996 to 203,300 in 2001. The number of people who learn an Aboriginal language as their mother tongue is now at 21% and only 13% spoke an Aboriginal language "most often in their home." [32]

Between 1986 and 2001, children aged 0 to 19 dropped from 41% to 32% of the total first language speakers which means that Aboriginal language speakers are ageing. Even more worrisome is the trend showing only 15% of Aboriginal children under five learned an Aboriginal mother tongue. [33]

While there are over 50 languages, Cree (39%), Inuktitut (15%), Ojibway (12%), Montagnais-Naskapi (5%), and Dene (5%) together make up over 76% of all mother tongue speakers. [34] This indicates that the survival of many other languages is threatened.

According to Mary Jane Norris,

> *Children are the future speakers of Aboriginal languages; their language outcomes are critical to the maintenance and revitalization of their languages. Language outcomes of children today have significant implications for the language status of future generations.*

> *According to the United Nations Educational Scientific and Cultural Organization (UNESCO), a language is considered endangered if it is not learned by at least 30% of children in a*

community. The 2001 Census indicated that only 15% of Aboriginal children in Canada under the age of five had learned an indigenous mother tongue. Children are the major source of growth for the Aboriginal mother tongue population in Canada. The decrease in the numbers of first-language speakers since 1996 attests to the impact of declining continuity. Lowered rates of language transmission to younger generations seem to be no longer offset by still relatively high levels of Aboriginal fertility.

According to UNESCO, Canada's Aboriginal languages are among the most endangered in the world. [35]

Norris points out that,

> *The increasing acquisition of Aboriginal languages as a second language, especially among youth, cannot be considered a substitute for learning it as a mother tongue. While second language acquisition can play an important role in slowing down language erosion and possible extinction, restoration of language transmission from one generation to the next requires an increase in the number of first-language speakers.*

THE ROLE OF EDUCATION

Current educational approaches are doing little to remedy the situation and often further impede the language opportunities of Aboriginal children and youth. Wilson noted that problems are posed when:

> *Let's say they study in Inuktitut up until Grade 3 and starting at Grade 4 they are expected to perform in English, which is their second*

language, as well as any other English speaking Canadian. This is one of the main causes of huge dropout rates. Berger described it very well in his report.

Wilson also observed that while the French-speaking community in Nunavut receives annual funding for French language,

> Inuktitut doesn't receive much funding. It's ironic that there are French schools, very well-funded, and there isn't a single Inuit school with Inuktitut as the main language.

Inuit Tapiriit Kanatami (ITK) has noted "The necessity for Inuit as well as English literacy and language learning to be provided throughout the educational systems cannot be overstated." [36]

Aboriginal teachers can serve as role models and cultural transmitters. Yet most Aboriginal students aged 15-24 did not have an Aboriginal teacher; only 32% of off-reserve First Nations youth had an Aboriginal teacher or aide. The figure was higher for Inuit in the Far North (81%).[37]

According to Wilson, both the materials and the instructors are critical for success in educating Inuit children and youth:

> In general, the main complaint is that the school program curriculum is quoted from a Southern curriculum, from Alberta let's say, and just applied in Nunavut without considering the cultural context and different language, anything. And the other thing is, there are no materials in Inuktitut developed.

> And, there aren't that many Inuit teachers at the high school level.

ITK has stressed the need for trained Inuit teachers and educators:

> The Inuit education systems are now unable to provide equitable and quality programs to their students. Also, considering the high student drop out rate, it is imperative that ways and means be developed to retain students to program completion with every possible mode of support and encouragement.[38]

Nonetheless, innovative approaches can be identified, says Wilson,

> Across the Inuit regions there are examples of excellent work done by Inuit educators who, despite the lack of resources, develop Inuit culture and knowledge-based teaching materials and there are young Inuit teachers who fully understand the importance of language and culture in education.

She also notes that McGill University has a very good program that prepares and trains Inuit teachers.

Budd points to sources of education beyond school teachers:

> I am really glad that we have that APTN Aboriginal TV station. Now there are programs. There is often Cree, Ojibway whatever, the languages. A couple of hours of native language. That is a good start. But even to start having that and having these elders bring that language back and always talking our language.

With many Aboriginal languages in danger, it is a struggle for Aboriginal children and youth when the dominant media and language of education is not Aboriginal.

CULTURAL PRESERVATION

As difficult as it is for many Aboriginal children and youth to preserve their languages, it is equally difficult to preserve culture, of which language is an integral part.

Wilson notes the irony of having to teach culture to a people who are living in it:

> It's kind of ironic in a way too, speaking of culture, that one has to teach culture to people who are this culture but certainly much of it comes down to the socio-economic situation in general. Overcrowding in houses, a huge unemployment rate, a generation gap related to residential schools' negative effect on people and the prevalence of English or French language in some communities.

Budd also comments on the damage inflicted by residential schools:

> That is how they decided to break us. They took away our kids to boarding school and kept them there for so many years. And even then would only give them a grade 8 education. They set them up for failure. They did not give them a grade 12 or university at that time because they did not want them to compete with the Europeans and take away the jobs.

Nonetheless, Budd notes a resurgence in Aboriginal culture,

> There are some groups that are stronger, getting stronger again and trying to pick themselves back up. They will take on that responsibility of looking after their tribe and their custom. We want the sweat lodge back. And it gets more defined, we want our language, how can we do that?

> There is one value now called the seven teachings. Did you hear about that? The creator created seven teachings and that they were lost. As the story goes, the grandmother turtle has brought the teachings back. Has given them through a ceremony and now they are spreading. The seven teachings are love carried by the eagle, buffalo carries respect, courage by the bear, honesty by the sabe (sasquatch), wisdom by the beaver, humility by the wolf and truth by the turtle.

But much more can be done according to Budd,

> We should have some elders in school. To have a respected native we can get the ball a little bit rolling by having elders in school. "Let's go talk to him."

> We also need a craft. What's wrong with setting up programs with native craft? I remember going to school on the reserve I was taught bead work. I was taught moccasin-making. An old man was brought in for us to make snow shoes. Another to show how to make teepees and canoes. Nobody knows how to make a canoe anymore or even pick wild rice—things that are natural and passing that on to the youth and work on the land. We are so

disconnected from the land. The land is our mother anyway.

Another thing I would like to mention. How do we involve families? It's sad how money or the lack of it affects programming. If funders really wanted to help, the money will always be there. The world is always changing and we're changing. I see a time when First Nations People will take the lead and solve its issues from within. That's how strong our Spirit is.

Eegeesiak adds that the gap in cultural education for Aboriginal children and youth is at least partially resource-driven with:

the schools not having the resources to teach things like Inuktitut. Of course there won't be any resources to teach our young people our culture from the school side. Some of our leaders are saying that it's too expensive to maintain, to sustain, traditional activities as well. People can't afford the gas, the fuel, the skidoos, and the boats to keep the tradition going. So it's not only education and training of cultural activities it's the expense of it as well.

From early learning initiatives to post secondary opportunities, to language and culture, education for Aboriginal children and youth is inadequately understood or resourced.

GOVERNANCE AND RESOURCES

Numerous reports and Aboriginal organizations over the years have stressed the importance of Aboriginal control or input into education for Aboriginal peoples; for collaboration, comprehensive, culturally relevant approaches and adequate resources.

As noted by the Royal Commission on Aboriginal Peoples:

Aboriginal people are well aware of the power of education. Greater control over their children's education has been a demand for at least three decades.

Parental involvement and local control of schools are standard practice in Canada—but not for Aboriginal people. Instead, they have long been the object of attempts by state and church authorities to use education to control and assimilate them, during the residential school era, certainly, but also, more subtly, today.

By seeking greater control over schooling, Aboriginal people are asking for no more than what other communities already have: the chance to say what kind of people their children will become.[39]

For the majority of Aboriginal people who live in urban settings, the challenges are profound. As MacPhee explains,

Many urban Aboriginal children are either assimiliated by the dominant culture or segregated to the periphery of the community. Alienated from their own culture, stripped of their sense of identity and self-esteem, many Aboriginal

families and their children are lead into a sense of hopelessness and despair.

The AFN has long indicated that funding for on-reserve expenditures including education has been frozen at 2% since 1996.[40] This despite the fact that:

> An analysis of the enrolment increases on-reserve shows that education funding would have had to increase by 3% a year from 1996 to 2003 to remain stable in terms of real (inflation adjusted) expenditure per student.[41]

Justice Murray Sinclair explains,

> *Certainly, we're getting to a point where the amount of assistance, for example, being provided to Aboriginal kids, both Métis and First Nations, who want to go to university is now being cut back. It's just at the point where the bulge in the population is starting to hit the university age and it's the worse time of all for governments to be cutting back on providing educational resources but they are doing it. So we're getting more and more Aboriginal youth who want to go into post-secondary facilities and advance themselves to get a higher degree of education and at the same time government is cutting back on the resources.*
>
> *And it's very neat the way they've done it. They give control over the decision-making for the resources for the First Nations community to the tribal council or the Métis agency and they say "you decide who gets this money" and then they limit the pot to what it was 10 years ago. So they are giving the same amount of money for education today that they were giving 5 or 10 years ago, but there are more kids who are making demands on it. So there are large numbers of First Nations students that I know of who just can't get financial assistance for*

school. So they're going to be frustrated, they're going to be under-educated and not be able to realize their own potential.

Dr. Nathan Matthew recently negociated a precedent setting tripartite education agreement among British Columbia First Nations, the Government of British Columbia and the Government of Canada.

As a result of these efforts Bill C-34: *An Act to provide for jurisdiction over education on First Nation lands in British Columbia* was passed by both the House of Commons and the Senate and received Royal Assent on December 12, 2006.[42]

According to Dr. Matthew, *"We have been working toward Indian control of Indian education since 1972. Specifically in B.C. we have been having discussions since the year 2000."*

There were a number of agreements and stages that led up to Bill C-34 being passed into law. Dr. Matthew says,

> *There are a couple of fundamental issues around jurisdiction and until we have a specific agreement like this we continue to be under the authority of the Minister of Indian Affairs. And that is something that we do not want. So, politically this moves us out from under the Indian Act and the influence of the Minister of Indian Affairs. It puts the responsibility for education in the hands of First Nation communities. By having the responsibility and control, the quality of education will grow.*

According to Dr. Matthew, First Nation jurisdiction over education will benefit First Nations children, families, and communities:

We will handle our own education, it will have parental input, and we will have community support. This will lead to a better quality of education and more relevant education with respect to culture and language.

It's one of the very few self-government agreements for education for First Nations in Canada, and it clearly sets out lawmaking authority for First Nations for Kindergarten to grade 12 on-reserve. We intended on having a more holistic, life-long learning perspective and decision making and authority but in the negotiations it was narrowed down to K-12 on-reserve. So, we have other work in post-secondary and early childhood education that we are working on, and in the K-12 area we are working on the implementation, and making sure that the governance structures that we have for First Nations are solid.

According to Wilson, the Government of Nunavut is currently working on an education act. It will serve as,

> *. . . a model for other territories and maybe help develop one national curriculum for teaching Inuktituk in all schools and adopting Inuktituk curriculum in general throughout the culture in all four regions.*

Ultimately, says Eegeesiak,

> *. . . a lot of the solutions are identified in terms of recommendations. Many have developed over the years. It is just a matter of partnering with government, the federal government in this case, I guess, and getting the resources to implement the recommendations.*

In other words, adds Wilson, *"It's time to act."*

IN SUMMARY

First Nations, Métis and Inuit children and youth en masse receive fewer educational opportunities compared to other Canadian children and youth, regardless of where they live. Nor does the education offered generally facilitate the learning and retention of Aboriginal languages and culture.

Disproportionately low Aboriginal rates of completion for secondary and post-secondary education can be traced to many factors, including systemic racism, socio-economic factors, lack of funding/resources and inadequate Aboriginal control or input into education. Statistics tell the story of increasing Aboriginal success in education where Aboriginal peoples are involved in determining Aboriginal education; this success would be all the greater were such initiatives adequately resourced. Given the young demographic of the Aboriginal population the time to act is now.

ABORIGINAL CHILD AND YOUTH HEALTH, WELLNESS AND SAFETY

Some of the highlights of the RHS report are the issue of overcrowding and how this affects children and youth health. We have high rates of allergies, asthma, and chronic ear infections. A lot of that can be related to housing conditions, and we also have a lot of mould in our homes. One of the things that I find so hard to believe in the year 2003 is that there are still homes within our communities where there is no running water or a toilet. Our children are being raised in those types of environments. To me that is one of the most astounding facts for 2003. According to the RHS survey 1 in 30 First Nations live in homes without running water, another factor that is hard to believe is that 32% of the population on-reserve feels their water is unsafe.

All that we are talking about here deals with people who are poverty stricken.

Jane Gray

Despite the fact that Canada is wealthy, with an enviable healthcare system in comparison to other nations, the health status of Aboriginal peoples remains substantially poorer than that of the general Canadian population.[1] Yet, health challenges in the Aboriginal community are also inevitably problems to be faced by Canada at large, particularly given an expanding and youthful Aboriginal population demographic. Perhaps more so than in any other area, the interconnectedness of the myriad factors underlying poor Aboriginal health and wellness are apparent, necessitating a holistic, comprehensive approach to remedying this inequality.

ABORIGINAL HEALTH AND WELLNESS

Given the growing and younger Aboriginal population, existing problems in Aboriginal health are only likely to increase in the future, if not adequately addressed in the present.

According to Dr. Valerie Gideon,

The First Nations population is significant, numbering over 700,000 people, which makes the population nation-wide larger than five provinces/territories. Statistics in a number of the provinces also indicate that the First Nations population is the fastest growing with the current medium age falling in the mid to late teens. As such, given the current health crisis, the status of First Nations health and the First Nations health system demands the attention of the federal government and of all Canadians.

Dr. Gideon explains,

First Nations perceive the state of their personal health as poorer than other Canadians. It is repeatedly documented that First Nations' life expectancy is 5 to 7 years lower, infant mortality 1.5 times higher, and a suicide rate 2.5 times higher than the Canadian public. These problems are in addition to the problems that the Canadian public also faces, such as waiting times and lack of coordination among health providers, services and patient information.

Unfortunately, the First Nations perception to which Dr. Gideon refers all too often reflects reality for many Aboriginal adults, children and youth.

ABORIGINAL CHILDREN & YOUTH: IN A "CRISIS STATE"

As the burgeoning Aboriginal youth population grows into adulthood, there will be major pressure on the health care system in relation to health-related behaviours and socio-demographics. In addition, these generational differences are just one indication of why health delivery systems that are relevant to the general Canadian population may not be relevant to Aboriginal peoples.

Aboriginal children and youth and their communities face numerous health-related challenges. According to Dr. Gideon,

The health of First Nation, Inuit, and Métis children and youth remains in a crisis state. In comparison to the Canadian public, these children and youth face much higher rates of chronic and communicable diseases, and are exposed to greater health risks because of poor housing, contaminated water and limited access to healthy foods and employment opportunities.

Despite the many differences among Aboriginal peoples, children and youth experience similar health challenges.

SNAPSHOT OF ABORIGINAL CHILD AND YOUTH WELLNESS

The following snapshot of Aboriginal child and youth wellness provides examples of the extent of those challenges:

- An infant mortality rate among Inuit in Nunavik (northern Quebec) of 24.9 deaths per 1,000 live births, and among First Nations of 6.4 deaths per 1,000.[2] Despite a promising decline in infant mortality, shown in Chart 5.1, levels of morbidity and mortality among First Nations children and youth on-reserve remain high throughout their first 18 years of life.

- More than half of First Nations children were either overweight (22%) or obese (36%).[3]

- Diabetes is another prevalent Aboriginal health problem. Rates of diabetes among Aboriginal people in Canada are three to five times higher than those of the general Canadian population. Aboriginal children are also now being diagnosed with type 2 diabetes.[4]

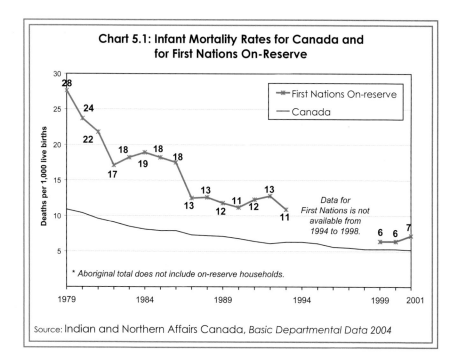

Chart 5.1: Infant Mortality Rates for Canada and for First Nations On-Reserve

Deaths per 1,000 live births

- First Nations On-reserve
- Canada

28, 24, 22, 17, 18, 19, 18, 18, 13, 13, 12, 11, 12, 13, 11, 6, 6, 7

Data for First Nations is not available from 1994 to 1998.

* Aboriginal total does not include on-reserve households.

1979   1984   1989   1994   1999   2001

Source: Indian and Northern Affairs Canada, *Basic Departmental Data 2004*

- 60% of on-reserve First Nations people between the ages of 18 and 34 currently smoke; 70% of Inuit in the north between the ages of 18 and 45 currently smoke and almost half of Inuit (46%) who smoke started smoking at age 14 or younger. The majority of on-reserve First Nations people who smoke (52%) started smoking between the ages of 13 and 16.[5]

- Aboriginal youth are at two to six times higher risk for alcohol related problems than their non-Aboriginal counterparts.[6]

- They use solvents more frequently than other Canadian youth. One in five Aboriginal youth has used solvents; one third of all users are under 15 and more than half of all solvent users began use before age 11.[7]

- First Nations and Métis youth are more likely to use all types of illicit drugs than non-Aboriginal youth, and Aboriginal youth begin using substances (tobacco, solvents, alcohol and cannabis) at a much earlier age.[8]

- Aboriginal communities are vulnerable to the devastating effects of crystal meth and other drugs because of geographic and social isolation, lack of economic opportunities, the loss of culture, identity and language that resulted from historic policies of assimilation.[9]

- First Nations youth have an elevated risk of suffering from a physical, developmental or learning disability, and behavioural or emotional problems. Fetal alcohol syndrome and fetal alcohol effects are responsible in many cases.[10]

- The most common causes of death for First Nations people aged 1 to 44 years was injury and poisoning. Among children under 10 years, deaths were primarily classified as unintentional (accidental). Potential years of life lost from injury was more than all other causes of death combined and was almost 3.5 times that of the Canadian rate.[11]

- The disability rate among First Nations children was found to be twice that of the general population (7.8% vs. 4.4%).[12]

- Aboriginal people in Canada continue to be over-represented in the HIV epidemic and are infected with HIV at a younger age compared to non-Aboriginal persons.[13] Aboriginal youth are over-represented in many of the populations most vulnerable to HIV infection, such as inner city populations, sex-trade workers and incarcerated populations.[14]

- Suicide rates are five to six times higher for First Nations youth than for non-Aboriginal youth. Suicide rates among Inuit youth are among the highest in the world, at 11 times the national average.[15]

- First Nation youth with a parent who attended residential school were more likely to ponder suicide (26% vs. 18%).[16]

- Suicide is clearly linked with depression and childhood sexual or physical abuse, all deemed to be significantly higher among the Aboriginal population than the non-Aboriginal population.[17]

- Girls in First Nations communities are twice as likely as boys to report feeling sad, blue, or depressed for two weeks or more over the previous year (44% vs. 22% of 15-17 year olds).[18]

- One of the more significant concerns of Inuit people is the negative impact of PCB's and mercury that pollute their environment and have a negative impact on Inuit infant health.[19]

In fact, Aboriginal children are at higher risk across almost all indicators of health.[20]

SUCCESS STORIES

However, there are some success stories. For example, breast feeding rates for children have risen.[21]

The First Nations Regional Longitudinal Health Survey (RHS) uncovered some success stories, says Jane Gray,

There is a positive component to our RHS as well, and this is part of the holistic approach. One of the positive things we have noticed is that the breastfeeding rates went up amongst our children. According to RHS, 3 in 5 (63%) children are breastfed. In 1997, only 50% of the children were breastfed. Another positive fact found in RHS is that 1 in 4 of our children understands a First Nation language well, and 1 in 5 speaks their own language fluently. This is important in building pride in being First Nation.

And the Aboriginal Head Start initiative is working. Designed to prepare young children for their school years, the program addresses their emotional, social, health, nutritional and psychological as well as educational needs. The program aims to enhance parenting skills and improve family relationships while fostering emotional and social development.

Those children who had enrolled in the program had a 12% rate of repeating a grade in school, compared to the non-enrolled rate of 19%.[22] As indicated by the success of the Head Start Program, the roots of wellness for Aboriginal children and youth are much broader and deeper than what is traditionally thought of as mainstream health.

ABORIGINAL WOMEN: WELLNESS AND SAFETY

The health and wellness of Aboriginal children and youth is closely related to the situation of their mothers, and the families and communities in which they are being raised. Aboriginal women do not share the same level of good health experienced by other Canadian women. In 2001, life expectancy was 71.7 years for Inuit women,

76.7 years for First Nations women and 77.7 years for Métis women, compared with 82.2 years for Canadian women in general.[23]

Aboriginal women have higher incidences of diabetes, tobacco addiction, and HIV/AIDS. They are also more likely to seek services to treat drug and alcohol abuse than are other Canadian women. Related are problems concerning fetal alcohol spectrum disorder (FASD) and family dysfunction and violence. Aboriginal women also have a suicide rate up to eight times that of other Canadian women, depending on age.[24] The sub-Canadian standard of health of Aboriginal women cannot be disassociated from other factors, including poverty and unemployment, family violence, poor housing and living conditions and the cost of quality food in remote communities.[25]

Aboriginal women's unequal status in Canadian society results in their increased vulnerability to exploitation and violence. Compared to other Canadian women, Aboriginal women are more than three times as likely to report that they have experienced some form of violence perpetrated by their spouse and Aboriginal women run eight times the risk of being killed by their spouse.[26] Twenty-four percent of Aboriginal women were assaulted by a current or former spouse during the 2004 General Social Survey five-year period, 1.3 times the rate for Aboriginal men (18%) and about three and a half times the rate for non-Aboriginal women and men.[27]

Aboriginal women's vulnerability to violence and sexual assault within their communities is fuelled by social and economic marginalization and a history of colonialist government policies including residential schools, which have disrupted relations between Aboriginal men and women and eroded cultural identity. The dispossession of status Indian women who married outside their communities and the removal of First Nations children to be educated in residential schools greatly contributed to the marginalization of Aboriginal women within both their communities and Canadian society.[28]

The abuse of alcohol and drugs, poverty and overcrowding in First Nations homes are also contributing factors to violence both on- and off-reserve. The absence of alternative housing arrangements is problematic for all Aboriginal women, noted most particularly for Inuit, while women in remote communities may face inadequate police response time.[29]

In the cities, Aboriginal women are at greater risk of violence and assault than all other Canadian women, arising from racist and sexist attitudes.[30] Discrimination and Aboriginal women's inequality in society contribute to a perception that they are easy targets; discriminatory and sexist policing has all too often rendered this perception reality. Aboriginal women aged 25-44 are five times more likely than other Canadian women of the same age to die of violence, and more than 500 Aboriginal women have gone missing or been murdered over the last 30 years.[31]

Social and economic marginalization combined with addictions and other factors, has led to Aboriginal women being highly overrepresented as sex trade workers; racism compounds the threat to safety and security faced by all such workers.[32]

These dire facts impact Aboriginal children and youth doubly; as the children of Aboriginal women who are frequently lone parents and as bystanders who may unwittingly get caught up in the cycle of violence, and end up abusers or victims of abuse themselves. Young Aboriginal women may already be experiencing the manifestations of systemic racism and gender inequality.

FIRST NATIONS REGIONAL LONGITUDINAL HEALTH SURVEY

The RHS is an important source of information in this Chapter. According to Gray, the RHS

> . . . is the only national [health] research initiative under complete First Nation control in Canada. It is not government, Statistics Canada, or university driven. It's driven by First Nations communities.

Accordingly, results of the RHS are more culturally sensitive to First Nation issues.

In conducting the survey, Gray works with ten regional coordinators to collect data at the national and regional level, representative of the adult, youth and child population on-reserve. Gray says RHS *"is the best and most reliable source of information for the First Nations population."* Further she says,

> *The questionnaire was developed with a cultural component; the questions were designed to be culturally sensitive to First Nation issues and realities. We work with a holistic cultural framework; the cultural component is integrated into everything we do. The cultural framework is based on the values and principles of First Nations and uses the four directions concept.*

> *When we did our data interpretation we took into consideration the reality and history of*

> *the people, and the reports have this context added in. This cultural framework makes the RHS unique and different from other research processes. We reported our information back to the communities using the four directions model of the medicine wheel (north, south, west, and east). It's not your standard medical model approach.*

> *It is important to mention the founding principles behind the RHS Code of Research Ethics; we refer to them as the First Nation Principles of OCAP— Ownership, Control, Access, and Possession. What this means is that First Nations are in control of their own research agenda, we own our information, we control how it's being used, we control how it's being accessed, and we possess our own information/ data. These are the fundamental principles of what we are all about. Simply said, RHS is about self-determination in the area of research.*

The RHS report highlights many of the health and wellness challenges identified for the First Nations community at large:

> *What we found is that if you didn't complete high school your average salary was $11,718 a year. 50.4% of children's fathers and 41.2% of their mothers didn't graduate high school. More than half of all adults on-reserve are not employed. RHS also has highlighted another reality; we have a high number of our First Nation kids repeating grades, especially amongst our young boys.*

> *There are also a lot of issues concerning weight amongst our children and youth. 58% of our children were either overweight or obese according to the International Body Mass Index standard. It is our 3-5 year olds that are really obese, and it is scary to think of the health impacts on them 20 years from now. If you think*

our rates of diabetes are high right now, can you imagine what they are going to be like 20 years from now? That is going to have a major impact on our healthcare services within the community and within hospital settings.

Another surprising finding from RHS is that among our youth, particularly young women, there are high rates of smoking. The smoking rates did go down from RHS in 1997 but our girls are smoking more than the boys. So, there are going to be impacts down the road for our people. These are the women that are going to be creating the next generation of children. There is also the whole issue of hypertension which is associated with smoking. So, add on another 20 years and what is our health data going to be like?

RHS also has found that there are a number of mental health issues amongst our youth. There are more thoughts of suicide among our youth when compared to the Canadian population. Communities need to start looking at the youth, what there needs are, what needs to be done, and start implementing their recommendations.

Gray also speaks about the difficulty of getting the RHS acknowledged, with the RHS undergoing independent review by Harvard University before it was accepted and recognized as a valid research process.

With regard to youth health, the RHS recommends specific strategies/interventions to improve the health and well-being of First Nations youth in the areas of language and culture, housing, education, self-esteem and resilience.[33]

The RHS findings also provide evidence says Dr. Gideon,

> *Supporting the need for strategies and interventions to target households and families, versus individuals, when these are aimed at improving the health and well-being of First Nations children and youth.*

"Ultimately", says Gray,

> *'Process' is every bit as important as 'products' with the RHS putting a face to the numbers in order to generate change in First Nations communities.*

SOCIAL DETERMINANTS

We must also turn a critical eye to the social determinants of health and the root causes behind the sub-Canadian standard for Aboriginal children and youth.

Aboriginal health cannot be disassociated from other factors, including poverty, lack of educational attainment and unemployment, family violence, overcrowded housing and poor living conditions, unsafe drinking water and the cost of quality food in remote communities.

Nor are any of the issues stand-alone; rather they are inextricably interconnected and indivisible from the systemic and pervasive nature of Aboriginal peoples' inequality in Canadian society. The social and economic marginalization of Aboriginal peoples is a key contributing factor in poor Aboriginal health. These root causes facilitate obesity, addictions, diabetes, chronic illness, depression and suicide, among others. Depression and behavioural problems frequently stem from socio-economic conditions, such as extreme poverty, combined with a loss of identity among Aboriginal children and youth, all too often culminating in suicide.

Poverty is one of the most significant problems amongst Métis, Inuit, and First Nations people contributing to poor health outcomes. For example, low income Métis families are particularly prevalent in Quebec, Manitoba, and Saskatchewan where one third of Métis children are living in low-income households.[34] In comparison to non-Aboriginal families, Métis, Inuit and First Nations families are more likely to be living in homes below the Canada Mortgage and Housing Corporation's housing standards.[35] In addition, lower average wages and lower levels of education for Aboriginal peoples contribute to this impoverished state.

As noted by Dr. Gideon,

> *Poverty among First Nations children in Canada—one in four compared to one in six Canadian children—is a shameful reality that Canada must face. A direct correlation has been shown by the RHS 2002/03 between family income, the level of overcrowding, poor nutrition and lower levels of physical activity and educational achievement among First Nations children and youth. Hence, comprehensive community development that reinforces the capacity of First Nations governments to respond to the needs of their community members is essential to achieve marked improvements in First Nations children's health and well-being.*

Aboriginal children and youth's substandard health is fuelled by marginalization and a history of colonialist government policies including residential schools, which have disrupted family relations and eroded cultural identity. Aboriginal children and youth today may be the victims of abuse, suffering the intergenerational impacts of residential schools, with their families unwittingly caught up in the cycle of violence.

HOLISTIC APPROACHES

Community-based health initiatives which take into account the systemic inequality of Aboriginal peoples and its root causes are fundamental to addressing the sub-par state of Aboriginal child and youth wellness. Use of the term "wellness" may conjure a more holistic approach to health, one that incorporates body, mind, spirit and intellect. This is reflective of the Aboriginal approach to wellbeing, one that involves personal and cultural continuity.

Culture, language, and traditions, although diverse among Inuit, Métis, and First Nations people, are considered an integral part of the holistic view of health held by Aboriginal peoples.[36] The physical, mental, spiritual, and emotional aspects of an individual are all interconnected. Thus, for example, the AFN vision of an effective health plan is a *"First Nations controlled and sustainable system that adopts a holistic, culturally appropriate approach."* The AFN also emphasizes the *"link between cultural continuity and self determination, and better health and health determinant outcomes"* for First Nations people.[37]

Aboriginal people have a *"rich tradition of healing and wellness practices,"* [38] and communities have demonstrated success in providing health services.[39] For example, Ontario's health access centres, funded by the Aboriginal Healing and Wellness Strategy, were found to highly improve access by 87% of urban and 64% of rural Aboriginal residents.[40] In addition, birthing centres in Nunavut and Nunavik have successfully integrated contemporary and traditional approaches.[41]

Unfortunately, many of the mental and emotional health issues affecting Aboriginal people are not understood holistically but are rather conceptualized in terms of the mainstream culture. Within the mainstream medical establishment too little is known and understood about Aboriginal wellness. By integrating mainstream medical wisdom with Aboriginal traditional knowledge, healing practices and holistic approaches, we can collaborate on a brighter future for Aboriginal children and youth, their communities, and all Canadians.

According to Dr. Gideon, in 2005 the AFN conducted an environmental scan of healthy living policy considerations, which revealed the following foundational components of a First Nations holistic health strategy:

- First Nations driven;
- Adopts a community health approach;
- Builds on best practices;
- Takes a holistic approach to healthy living;
- Seeks adequate funding to support infrastructure, programs and resources in animating the strategy; and is,
- Inclusive of solutions around determinant of health issues specific to First Nations.

Dr. Cathy Richardson notes the role of a holistic approach in supporting victims of violence:

I do a lot of work to support victims of violence but my approach is a bit broader than many of the people who work in transition houses, for example.

My work has involved drawing on Métis, but also in a broader sense, what I would call Indigenous wellness. Using victims' knowledge looking at how communities stayed alive through times of severe cultural attacks. Going through the Colonial or settlement period, they were getting pushed off the land and dispersed. Trying to get a sense of what people did then to stay safe or connected or alive and then apply some of that knowledge to wellness today.

You start having conversations with people about how they've made it this far. You can say, "Well how is it that your friends might have died in that situation but you stayed alive?" Or, you know "You've made it this far, you're not in prison." So looking at those kinds of things and then building that knowledge into programming. Violence prevention is one of my biggest areas and I think that also really leads to prevention and keeping children out of child welfare.

Prevention constitutes a significant component of the general holistic philosophy of care in Aboriginal communities. Health services must include access to culturally appropriate programs for prevention, targeting children and youth and building capacity within Aboriginal organizations and communities. For example, if a person does not begin the use of tobacco, alcohol, or illegal substances between the ages of 15 and 24, it is considered highly unlikely they will ever do so.[42] Prioritizing prevention is not only fiscally sound, but also a humanitarian response to child and youth wellness, which should be viewed on a continuum leading to healthy adulthood.

ACCESSIBILITY

To address the pressing health needs of Aboriginal children and youth, health services must be made more accessible. Health services are a jurisdictional maze, with federal government responsible for primary health care services and non-insured health benefits coverage for status Indians and Inuit in Canada, regardless of residence. Provincial and territorial governments provide health services for Métis and non-status Indians, but also provide services such as doctors and hospitals to status Indians and Inuit. In order to effectively deliver an Aboriginal holistic approach, the complex jurisdictional issues—particularly those faced by non-status Indians living off reserve and by Métis—must be resolved.

Many Inuit experience problems accessing even mainstream health services in the North, due to a shortage of services at the local level, and a general lack of specialized services which often forces those needing treatment to leave their communities. As noted by the Inuit Tapiriit Kanatami (ITK), some Inuit have to travel thousands of kilometers to get treatment as patients or to be educated as health care providers.[43] Other Aboriginal groups living in the North, such as Métis with the Labrador Métis Nation, face similar problems accessing mainstream health services.[44]

Further, there is a gap in culturally appropriate health services for the rapidly growing urban Aboriginal population, who often have access only to mainstream programs. Métis and non-status Indian children and youth further experience lack of access to programs provided by the federal government through the Non-Insured Health Benefits regime of Health Canada. It is delivered to status Indians and Inuit groups, but not to non-status Indians and Métis peoples even though they may be in the same families as those who are eligible.

Inuit in urban centres often do not have access to federal government health programs and in many programs the higher cost of living in the North is not taken into account. First Nations may find they have to return to their reserve to access federally funded programs, while on-reserve, facilities such as detox/addiction treatment are limited.[45]

Since 1997-98, the federal government has maintained a 2% cap on spending increases for core services which includes all social programming provided to First Nations communities. Similarly, since 1996-97, the Indian health envelope, containing all core programs of the First Nations and Inuit Health Branch of Health Canada has been generally capped at 3% annually.[46]

According to Dr. Gideon,

> These caps ignore basic cost drivers such as population growth, ageing, and inflation. These caps also represent less than one-third of the average 6.6% increase that most Canadians will enjoy through the Canada Health and Social Transfers in each of the next five years.
>
> When adjusted for inflation and population growth over time, the total budget for INAC has decreased by 3.5% since 1999-2000. Core program budgets, such as social development and capital facilities and maintenance, have decreased by almost 13% since 1999-2000. This health and social fiscal imbalance has resulted in a gradual impoverishment of

community budgets. If communities had been funded in alignment with population growth and inflation, their budgets would be 45.5% higher than they are today."

The Assembly of First Nations projects a shortfall of close to $2 billion in federal health funding for First Nations over the next five years. This translates to an average gap for individual First Nations communities of 9% in 2006/07 and 14% in 2007/08.

Dr. Gideon stresses that,

. . . more funding is required for First Nations health programs and services as well as First Nations health organizations and better co-ordination and communication between the different levels of government. This would apply as well to funding and organizations targetting other Aboriginal people.

PARTNERING THE WAY FORWARD

In developing health programs for Aboriginal peoples it is important to consider their unique history, geographic location, and cultures. For example, ITK states that most federal initiatives have taken a pan-Canadian or pan-Aboriginal approach and have not developed Inuit-specific strategies. This impacts the success of these strategies in Inuit communities.[47] Thus, health programs designed by Inuit, Métis, and First Nations will be more accessible to these peoples.

According to Dr. Gideon,

A First Nations-specific approach is required to address the impact that historical factors have played and continue to play on the physical,

mental, emotional and spiritual health and well-being of First Nations children and youth in Canada. A flexible and holistic strategy would respond to the diversity among 633 First Nations communities across Canada in order for concrete, positive health outcomes to be achieved and the gap to be closed in health disparities between First Nations and other Canadians.

Not only must the approach be contextual and specific, but says Dr. Gideon,

The First Nations' health crisis will not be effectively addressed without the support of the federal and provincial/territorial governments. This is attributable to the First Nations-Crown fiduciary relationship as well as the complex cross-jurisdictional issues as they pertain to health service delivery to First Nations citizens, in or out of the community. There are inter-jurisdictional challenges to ensuring equitable access of First Nations communities to provincial/territorial services, and therefore, achieving a standard of care enjoyed by most Canadians.

"Equally," notes Dr. Gideon,

First Nations governments must exercise some jurisdiction in health service delivery; said jurisdiction is derived from First Nations' inherent right of self-government[48] and Indian Act by-law making powers.[49]

First Nations governments should be seen as partners in cross-jurisdictional health care approaches. *"In many cases they already are,"* adds Dr. Gideon,

More than 50% of First Nations communities have taken over the administration of their

health programs and services. Many First Nations tribal councils, communities, regional and national organizations (including the AFN) have youth councils that provide them with advice on the design and delivery of policies, programs and services.

In order to address the rather daunting challenges facing Aboriginal child and youth wellness says Gray, *"health promotion and public health is one area where funding has been cut, there needs to be a stronger focus on this."*

Aboriginal children, youth and adults will be better educated and informed in an environment of Aboriginal ownership of Aboriginal health. Initiatives such as the RHS invest in a process that is effective, accountable and produces reliable community based data. As noted by Dr. Gideon, long term, sustainable funding is required so that the RHS can track changes over time and effect policy change at the national level. Just as importantly, Jane Gray adds,

> *If you speak with the people, we know what we want, we know what we need, just listen to us, and implement it, instead of making decisions without First Nations involvement.*

Ultimately, key to any holistic program and policy development or Aboriginal control of wellness is consultation with the First Nations, Métis and Inuit peoples who require input; First Nations, Métis and Inuit women in particular want their voices heard in the process.

IN SUMMARY

Given Aboriginal demographics, existing problems in Aboriginal health are only likely to increase in the future, with children at high risk across almost all indicators of wellness. The health and wellness of Aboriginal children and youth is closely related to the health and safety of their mothers, families and communities.

Aboriginal health cannot be disassociated from other socio-economic factors. Holistic community-based health initiatives which take into account the systemic inequality of Aboriginal peoples and its root causes are fundamental to addressing Aboriginal child and youth wellness, incorporating body, mind, spirit and intellect.

To address the pressing health needs of Aboriginal children and youth, health services must be made more accessible, be culturally appropriate and adequately funded and prioritize prevention. Aboriginal peoples and governments should be seen as partners in cross-jurisdictional health care approaches in an environment of Aboriginal ownership of Aboriginal health, inclusive of the voices of Aboriginal women.

CHAPTER 6

HOUSING AND ABORIGINAL CHILDREN AND YOUTH

Now, I understand what you're saying in terms of looking at housing as a key factor that affects the development of children and youth. That's an honourable undertaking you might say, but I always insist that people try to overcome the western European approach of categorizing and individualizing various areas of social existence. You have social control. You have the related criminal justice system. So you have the judge and the policemen, lawyer and so on. Then you have the church and all its related exercises. Then you have the schools, universities and so on. And they don't seem to be really related. I have to remind people that our traditional approach to our existence has been based on recognition that everything is related and inter-related and I don't think you can really get away from that. In that context, then, I would not choose to speak of how housing, by itself, affects children and youth. But I think we have to take the approach that housing is one of the key and basic essentials of life.

Charlie Hill

No study of Aboriginal children and youth is complete without examining the effect of poor housing on the conditions of family life, wellness, education, employment and numerous other interconnected factors. Inadequate Aboriginal housing can be viewed as both cause and effect of poverty, low educational attainment, high unemployment rates, poor health and outcomes involving children in care and the justice system.

ABORIGINAL HOUSING

As established in other Chapters, Canada's Aboriginal population is younger and growing at a faster rate than the total population. This factor contributes to an even greater need for new housing. Additionally, some Aboriginal households require housing for an extended family which generates specific housing needs.

Another important consideration which is part cause and part effect of the housing crisis is the demographic trend indicating that Aboriginal people are changing residences within cities and in and out of cities at a more frequent rate than the overall population.

This high rate of churn among the urban Aboriginal population is emerging to have adverse effects on individuals, families, communities and service providers. As noted in one recent study:

> For example, many social programs that provide services to urban Aboriginal populations, such as health, family support and counseling, and education, are designed on a neighbourhood basis to ensure a coordinated response to multi--faceted family and individual needs. Frequent mobility among Aboriginal families can result in discontinuity or disruption of service provision, with negative consequences for the family and service provision agencies. Discontinuity in service provision can be especially pronounced among high-need families such as those of lone female parents, who are among the most mobile, yet often in the most need.[1]

As the Independent Indigenous Submission to the United Nations Committee on Economic, Social, and Cultural Rights in Response to Canada's Periodic Reports has noted,

> The issue of Aboriginal housing is not simply a matter of differences in living standards. Overcrowded and dilapidated houses pose a significant threat to the physical health of Aboriginal people to TB, diabetes, and obesity. Psychologically inadequate housing among Aboriginals reinforces a sense of marginalization and hopelessness. Furthermore adequate and affordable housing is essential to the stability children need to perform well in school; the need to move frequently hurts a child's social and academic development.[2]

Aboriginal housing needs must be viewed holistically; all too often however, they are not,

nor do housing programs/policies for Aboriginal peoples even provide adequate shelter.

ABORIGINAL HOUSEHOLDS (NON-RESERVE)

While the percentage of Aboriginal households in need has declined since 1996, it remained extremely high at 25% of all households in 2001. The absolute number of households in core need has risen from almost 70,000 to 74,000 from 1996 to 2001. Inuit households, as of 2001, were twice as likely to fall into core housing need as non-Aboriginal households.[3]

> *Households that have to spend more than 30% of their income to find adequate and suitable housing in their local housing market are considered to be in core housing need. Adequate housing means the dwelling has basic plumbing facilities and is not in need of major repair. Suitable housing means there are enough bedrooms for the size and make-up—age and sex—of the family.[4]*

Housing costs are greater as a percentage of income for Aboriginal people, mainly because, on average, Aboriginal household incomes lag behind those of non-Aboriginal households.

According to the 2001 Census, Aboriginal households reported an average 19.9% less than non-Aboriginal households. Yet Aboriginal households average shelter costs ($705) were only 8% lower than the average shelter costs ($766) of non-Aboriginal households. As a result, Aboriginal households spent more of their income on shelter relative to non-Aboriginal households, and a greater percentage fell into core housing need.[5]

At the same time that Aboriginal people spend more of their income on housing than average, the quality of Aboriginal housing is far inferior. In an examination of non-reserve housing, the Canadian Mortgage and Housing Corporation (CMHC) showed while non-reserve Aboriginal families represent only 2.8% of all families they make up 4.8% of those in core housing need. And this rises to over 22% in Manitoba and Saskatchewan, where about 10% of all households are Aboriginal.[6]

In large cities the housing need is even greater than in small urban centres. Almost 25% of Aboriginal households in census metropolitan areas and census agglomerations[7] were in core need in 2001 compared to 20% in small urban centres.[8]

Inuit people have been particularly hard hit in housing as funding is often apportioned by population numbers and as a small number of all Aboriginal peoples, Inuit often receive little money. Lack of local materials for housing as well as high transportation costs make housing construction even more expensive than in other areas.

Inuit are most likely to face overcrowding. In 2001, 20% of Inuit households were crowded followed by 10% for First Nations on-reserve and only 2% for the non-Aboriginal population.[9]

As Okalik Eegeesiak commented, *"it is kind of hard to study for anything when you have 3 or 4 generations living in one house."* Eegeesiak adds that *"with so many people living in the house and poor circulation that compounds the health status of everybody in the house."*

Maria Wilson adds,

> I think when speaking of Inuit and the north, most Canadians do not realize how different it is to do anything there. It's very expensive to bring building materials if one has to fly everything in. It is estimated that $9 billion is required to meet current need for housing in Nunavut. So how much of it is actually to buy building supplies and how much is to pay to bring it all into communities? And the population growth as you may have heard, 60% of the population is under the age of 25.

ITK has linked overcrowding to poor health especially for infants and to the transmission of infectious diseases such as tuberculosis (25 times the Canadian average for Inuit) as well as increasing the risk of injuries, mental health problems, family tension and violence. *"These stressors are powerful triggers for negative coping behaviors such as dependence on alcohol and drugs."* [10] A report prepared for ITK also noted that *"many Inuit offenders had difficult home environments during childhood, including exposure to violence and substance abuse."* [11]

Overcrowding for children leads to stressful homes and no space to study, skipping school more often and poorer education results. Overcrowding is a factor contributing to spousal abuse and other crime as well.

Alastair MacPhee, a childcare expert with the Congress of Aboriginal Peoples sums it ups succinctly:

> Access to good quality housing is essential for the well-being of Aboriginal children and the federal government should undertake a national housing strategy for all Aboriginal peoples.

HOMELESSNESS

Young people make up a crucial component of the homeless population and Aboriginal youth are overrepresented in this group. Studies indicate Aboriginal people as a whole are over-represented among all homeless people *"in every major city where statistics are available."* [12] In the North and in other rural areas the problem is often hidden and overcrowding or "couch surfing" are the methods by which it is concealed.

As noted by Dr. Cathy Richardson, a Métis psychologist, *"So what are people on the lower end doing? Many of these people are becoming homeless and that certainly is affecting a lot of Métis."*

Interviews conducted with Aboriginal street youth for the Royal Commission on Aboriginal Peoples (RCAP) found that for Aboriginal youth, their cultural

background, history, structural conditions and experience on the street were different from other street youth. Many experienced racism, in addition to the stigma encountered by all street people. The youth also spoke of identity confusion and self-hatred, dislocation from home, difficulty in reunification and ignorance of Aboriginal rights, history and culture.[13]

Some of the key urban indicators are:

- Calgary: Aboriginal people are 2% of the city's population but 17% of the homeless population, as shown in Chart 6.1;

- Edmonton: Aboriginal people are 4% of the city's population but about 37% of the homeless population;

- A 2001 CMHC study noted overrepresentation of Aboriginal

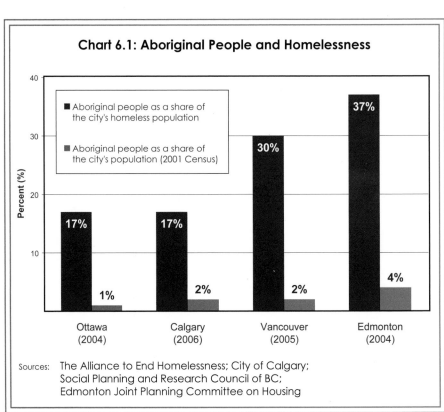

Chart 6.1: Aboriginal People and Homelessness

Legend:
- Aboriginal people as a share of the city's homeless population
- Aboriginal people as a share of the city's population (2001 Census)

	Ottawa (2004)	Calgary (2006)	Vancouver (2005)	Edmonton (2004)
Homeless population	17%	17%	30%	37%
City's population	1%	2%	2%	4%

Sources: The Alliance to End Homelessness; City of Calgary; Social Planning and Research Council of BC; Edmonton Joint Planning Committee on Housing

homeless youth particularly in Vancouver, Edmonton, Prince Albert, Saskatoon, Winnipeg, Toronto and Ottawa;[14]

- Ottawa: Aboriginal youth are 18% of the population of homeless male youth and 19% of homeless female youth, but only 2% of the population of Ottawa is Aboriginal.[15]

Garry Jobin observes:

A lot of our kids are dealing with homelessness. So, you have to know all the community agencies. If you're dealing with a kid that's kicked out on the street at 1:30 in the morning and is at the corner of Main and Hastings with all his clothes, you need to come in and know how to deal with that right away, and know who to call to get that young person housing, or you're going to lose them immediately.

Adds Charlie Hill:

You have to admit, and the research supports the fact, that Aboriginal people are the worst housed in Canada. There are programs that exist that were helpful but they were capped. Like the CMHC cap on new social housing in 1993. It was a successful program. The membership of the National Aboriginal Housing Association acquired about 11,000 housing units up until '93 but after that then there was a waiting list at the time but it has grown and grown. More and more people have become homeless. Homeless people start to include single-parents and families then it's really time to take a hard look at how come this is resulting. Now this isn't just limited to Aboriginal peoples. But the Aboriginal people are the worst of the worst.

After 1993, the existing subsidies at that time still continued except when the mortgages are terminating, then there's no more subsidy

so then the rents have to go up which has an impact on the families. In that case, it's a vicious circle.

Aboriginal youth are overrepresented among the homeless population in Canada. Given the demographics of a burgeoning youthful Aboriginal population combined with a shortage of adequate Aboriginal housing there is an immediate need for increased housing supports, or the Aboriginal homeless population may be expected to grow.

FIRST NATIONS ON-RESERVE

According to Hill, between housing on- and off-reserve,

Well there's not all that much difference. If you've got the economic base, you can support a house. Without the economic base you'll find it very, very hard to support a house. I'm not talking about a home, I'm talking about houses.

The major difference, of course, is the type of tenure. The fact that Canada holds the title to the land. I mean I don't know how they arrived at that. They came over and said, "This is our land but you can stay here if you want." It seems kind of ironic, but anyway, that's what happened and they in fact put us on reserves. People say that was to protect us, but it wasn't really. They fully expected us to die off as a people. If we wanted to leave the reserve and live elsewhere then we had to become what they call enfranchised and you had to pretend that you were not an "Indian." And so when people say, ". . . well, yeah, you chose to go and live on the reserves," that's not true. We were forced to go on the reserves and if you look around anyplace right now, it's all the worst land and we were forced into those territories.

> **A lot of people don't know that up until 1951, we had to have passes to leave the reserve.**
>
> Charlie Hill

CMHC noted that in 2001, 22.5% of on-reserve Aboriginal households were living in inadequate housing and in core housing need compared to 2.5% of non-Aboriginal households.[16]

The federal government has openly acknowledged the shortfall in reserve housing. In October 2006, INAC reported:

> Overcrowding and inadequate housing are of particular concern on-reserve, where there is a current housing shortage of between 20,000 and 35,000 units. The shortfall is growing by an estimated 2,200 units a year.[17]

CMHC noted that,

> As of March 2004, INAC reported a total of 95,479 dwelling units on-reserve, of which 16,878 required major repairs and 5,199 needed replacement. On-reserve housing shortages are currently estimated at 20,000 units, with an additional 4,500 new units needed annually to meet the requirements of new households.[18]

In recent years, in spite of these pressing needs, new on-reserve housing has declined or stagnated. In 2002-03 only 1,889 homes were built, down from 4,254 in 1993-94. The number of renovated dwellings has barely changed, from 4,126 in 1993-94 to 4,224 in 2002-03.[19]

Housing challenges include such inexcusable conditions as bad water and lack of sewage services. Indeed, the AFN has indicated,

> Currently [in 2006], almost 12% of First Nations communities have to boil their drinking water. Six percent of First Nations homes—over 5,000 homes, are without sewage services. Almost 1,600 homes lack hot water, cold water or flushing toilets.[20]

There were 89 First Nations communities under either "boil water" or "do not drink" advisories as of June 8, 2007.[21]

These conditions have negative effects that go beyond the physical health of the individual and extend to all elements of community wellness.

ABORIGINAL WOMEN AND HOUSING

Many First Nations women and their children face a particular legal issue in terms of housing.

Arising from the distribution of powers in *The Constitution Act, 1867*,[22] provincial or territorial law governs how assets of a marriage or common-law relationship are to be divided upon breakdown, including real property such as a house. The legislation generally provides for equal division between spouses.

However, these laws do not apply on-reserve as a result of subsection 91(24) of *The Constitution Act, 1867* which gives the federal government exclusive law-making authority over "Indians, and lands reserved for the Indians." This has been interpreted to mean that provincial and territorial matrimonial property laws do not apply to real property on-reserve. Since there are no federal provisions in the *Indian Act*[23] or elsewhere that fill in this matrimonial property gap, people living on-reserve generally have no legal system for resolving issues relating to land and houses upon a breakdown of their relationship.

Thus, First Nations women currently have no right in law to certain assets on-reserve where their marriage breaks down, unlike all other women in Canada; they and their children are therefore left with no legal claim to occupy the family residence. They may be forced to leave the matrimonial home and due to acute housing shortages, may also have to leave the reserve. Where family violence is involved, the woman and her children are rendered all the more vulnerable by this gap; sometimes remaining with the abuser for lack of an alternative.[24]

The human rights of First Nations women and their children are violated and they are discriminated against when they are unable to exercise rights they would have off-reserve.[25]

First Nations women want an avenue of redress and effective enforcement mechanisms for matrimonial matters involving real property on-reserve. Some Aboriginal people want the repeal of provisions in the *Canadian Human Rights Act*[26] preventing its protections from applying on-reserve. That would allow women some recourse if they believed a band Council's decision involving housing was discriminatory.

As Dr. Richardson observes, for Aboriginal women everywhere, violence, poverty and housing are closely linked,

> *. . . courts are deciding that if a woman is in a transition house because she had to leave her family home that is pretty unstable so often they would decide to put children with the assaulting spouse, the father, the child's Dad, because*

> *he might still have a home. So women are bearing a disproportionate responsibility for violence in families which is often used against them. So again, the issues of being vulnerable or subjected to violence they often relate to housing that is safe. You don't have a good place to live; you know children are removed from mothers due to poverty as well as being the victims of violence. For me, I would call that another human rights abuse.*

> *These issues are all related to violence and child welfare, human rights and how we are dealing with families.*

It is also noteworthy that Inuit women are often tenants of their homes, with the man's name on the lease, also resulting in great difficulty in removing a male perpetrator of violence from the home.[27]

LONE PARENTING

As well, Aboriginal women are more likely to be lone parents compared to non-Aboriginal women. This means more will be in core housing need due to high urban housing costs for single income families. Young women are often the most affected as lone parents. Nearly half (47%) of Aboriginal lone parents experience core housing needs as evidenced by Chart 6.2.

Dr. Richardson observes the change in Métis family structures:

> *So what happened, in a very short time our families moved from being what we would call extended families or living more communally both in communities but within houses it was quite normal that grandparents might live with a family or an aunt or uncle. And so we moved from that situation maybe quite quickly to a*

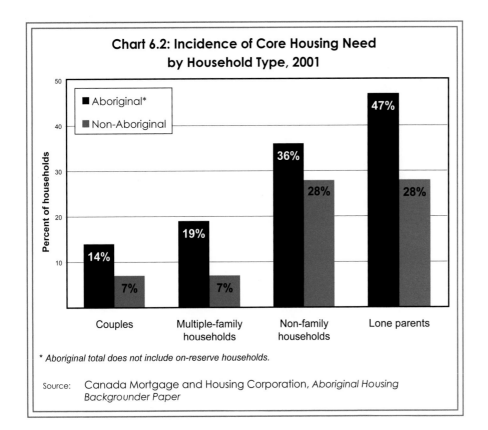

Chart 6.2: Incidence of Core Housing Need by Household Type, 2001

Percent of households

- Aboriginal*
- Non-Aboriginal

Couples	Multiple-family households	Non-family households	Lone parents
14% / 7%	19% / 7%	36% / 28%	47% / 28%

* Aboriginal total does not include on-reserve households.

Source: Canada Mortgage and Housing Corporation, *Aboriginal Housing Backgrounder Paper*

support, and family support and for communities. Those kinds of things could really be supported in advance through proper community-based housing.

Inadequate housing, family violence and underlying poverty issues are closely inter-related with Aboriginal children being taken into care as discussed more fully in that Chapter.

COMPREHENSIVE APPROACHES

As with all indicators of Aboriginal child and youth poverty, housing does not stand alone but must rather be viewed as interconnected to all other elements of the experience of Aboriginal peoples.

Hill notes,

> *So I mentioned the social aspects, the cultural-linguistic aspect, the economic aspect and the education aspect. All of these play a part in the success or lack of success in terms of housing.*
>
> *Over and above that is the whole question of racism that still exists.*
>
> *It's not just housing. You can't isolate housing and say that if you've got a good house that things will be great. There's this kind of stuff that you have to put up. There's that fact that the*

period of a nuclear family to a time when many of our families actually now are single-parent families living in urban settings or in small resource towns, so quite vulnerable to the flux of industries and facing a lot of issues related to poverty.

So when I think of what are the issues, well one issue certainly is housing. Architecture has never really helped the Métis, since 1885. So when families come to a city like Vancouver and they need to get an apartment, often it is one-bedroom where a mother will live with her children. And it's really hard to find apartments that are suitable for larger groups of people like an extended family. So I think housing is seriously related to other issues that link isolation, the need for quality childcare, peer

people, by and large, don't have any economic base with most of them coming from isolated communities so there's a language barrier. Low education.

But there's racism on top of everything else.

The result, Hill notes, is that Aboriginal people who do obtain a well-paying job and move into a neighbourhood that's "*all WASP*," often run into discrimination, while what usually happens is that Aboriginal people wind up in the worst housing in a city:

> *. . . that lends itself to this repression and being put into a ghetto-type of situation. So if you're forced into a negative housing situation, there's overcrowding, there's a struggle to pay the rent, because you can't get a good job and there's also the social repression. One more thing is that where there is a low-rent housing situation, usually that brings with it a bunch of other social ills. People who have not had a great opportunity whether they're white, Indian or black or what. This in turn lends itself to fostering not a very good attitude in terms of social responsibility. That's a nice way of saying there's a lot of troublemakers that hang around in low-rent areas. Now, this is not stereotyping, it's through experience.*

> *Having said that, you still want to hang out with your own people. You don't want to abandon your own people and go and try to live elsewhere because you're not well-received. You get pretty darn lonely so you stay with your people, your culture. I think that it is very important that our people start speaking up more for themselves.*

As always, funding, intergovernmental co-operation and Aboriginal control are major factors in the success or lack thereof in Aboriginal housing. According to Hill:

> *There's two things that I recommend that are essential. One is the increase of resources to help us acquire more housing units but the other thing is that it is essential that we be recognized as a people who can support ourselves in terms of administering houses and so on. I guess putting it another way is, Indian-controlled or Aboriginal control over their housing program.*

And a holistic approach to housing means addressing more than just Aboriginal people having a place to call home, says Hill:

> *One of the things that the Urban Native Housing Program incorporated into its activities was the role of tenant counsellor. I think this role is one of the keys and is one of the major differences between the mainstream housing and the Aboriginal housing is that we do have tenant counsellors.*

> *I think that the tenant counselling is one aspect but there also have to be special provisions made to provide counselling for the kids by other Aboriginal people. I mean education that will bring to the attention of our Aboriginal kids the fact that all of this stuff has happened but here we are and we have to make a fresh start. To help them understand why people are like they are on one hand, but why they are treated the way they are on the other.*

> *So, with regards to the youth I mean we are all children at one time, we were youth and we are adults. The difference is that we get to be bigger and stronger and you can start acting out. The one thing that I know has been instrumental in helping a lot of people find their feet again is their re-grasp or the revitalization of traditional teachings in their day-to-day life. I think that*

this is one of the areas that really has to be stressed.

Of course the housing groups are not in a position to provide that kind of instruction but if the tenant-counsellor position was either expanded or rendered more specific to dealing with children and youth then that might be one element that could be incorporated into the day-to-day activities of the tenant counsellor or person who is supposed to work with the tenants.

In addition to policy/program approaches pertaining to tenancy, says Hill,

Some people over the years have been able to move into well-paying jobs so they do have an economic base. I think that many are now in a position where they could carry mortgages if they don't have enough money to pay to buy a house outright so I think this is the other area the federal government should really look at. In devising ways, working with banks and real estate people to give Aboriginal people a break in terms of relief in terms of interest and things like that so that would help them to enter the home ownership area. I think that home ownership, in turn, makes a person feel better which is passed along to the kids but also people, non-native people start taking a different view, "Oh they have a house, they're just like us." But we're not like them but we have to live in the same environment.

Keep in mind, the other thing is that we have been specifically excluded in the sharing of the resources of this country. The resources have been turned over directly to the provincial governments and it has only been recently, like the diamond mines, where our people have really insisted that they have a share of the resources that are extracted. In this context, if

we could share the resources that are extracted then our people would then be, in fact, better-off and I think you have to admit that one reason Canadians have been well-off is because they had access and they took all the resources. So we're only a drop in the bucket in terms of population so it would be a simple matter to share some of the benefits from various resources which in turn then would help housing which in turn would help the kids.

The well-being and future prospects for Aboriginal children and youth are so tied to housing that only a comprehensive long-term approach will fill the need.

IN SUMMARY

Aboriginal housing is substandard and inadequate at rates disproportionate to that experienced by the non-Aboriginal population; Aboriginal people and youth particularly are also over-represented in the homeless population.

As with all indicators of Aboriginal child and youth poverty, housing does not stand alone but must rather be viewed as interconnected to all other elements of the experience of Aboriginal peoples, including racism and discrimination. Aboriginal housing issues must be approached through a holistic strategy. Adequate funding, intergovernmental co-operation, collaboration with Aboriginal communities and a focus on community economic development are all important for housing adequacy and sustainability.

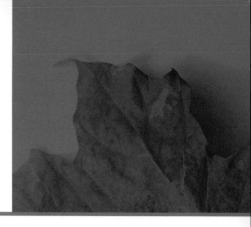

CHAPTER 7

ABORIGINAL CHILDREN AND YOUTH "IN CARE"

> *So here at Métis Services, my work is guided by the memory of a young boy named Richard Cardinal who was from Fort Chipewayan. By the time he was a young adolescent he had been in over 13 foster homes and he finally hanged himself in the backyard of one of the homes in Alberta and he said,*
> *"I just can't take this any more, I'm just so tired of waiting for love."*
> *And one of the things that showed to me is that I think you can measure the civilization of a country by how well it treats its most vulnerable citizens. And so for me, our most vulnerable citizens are the forgotten children who are in foster care.*
>
> Dr. Cathy Richardson

First Nation, Métis, and Inuit people of Canada have prolonged histories of their children being forcibly removed from their homes and communities due to federal, provincial, and territorial government policies. There are more First Nations children in care today than at any time in Canadian history. Policies based on Eurocentric views of child rearing have had a destructive effect on First Nation, Inuit, and Métis peoples.

A HISTORY OF "IN CARE"

RESIDENTIAL SCHOOLS AND THE SIXTIES SCOOP

In Canada from the 1800s to 1996 the Canadian government joined forces with church groups in an attempt to "eliminate any vestige of Aboriginality" through mandated Aboriginal attendance at residential schools.[1] Aboriginal children were removed from their homes for the purposes of assimilation.

The residential school experiment was an abysmal failure where Aboriginal children were frequently inflicted with physical, mental, sexual and spiritual abuse, and many died from disease or malnutrition.[2] As adults, many residential school survivors describe the prolonged effect residential school experience had on them such as an inability to bond with others, ineffective parenting skills, and use of drugs and alcohol to dull the pain of negative memories.[3] As a result the next generation of Aboriginal children in Canada did not fare any better, experiencing what is often referred to as the intergenerational effects of residential schools.

As noted by Charlie Hill,

> The other thing is that you've heard of quote, "traumatic stress," and I was talking with an elder who was reading about that and it suddenly dawned on him, and I fully agree, that there has been the passing down of various loads or degrees of post traumatic stress. Generation after generation so that we wind up with this entire burden on our people as they exist today. On top of that there are the legal restraints that required our children be taken away. You're very familiar with the residential school system and so on. I've often asked people of western European culture if I and a bunch of other Native people came in and took your small children away and you don't know whether you are ever going to see them again, well you wouldn't stand for it. We didn't stand for it, but we were outnumbered. This had a terrible impact on our people.

The impact Hill describes on First Nations was felt equally by Inuit families whose children were also sent to residential schools.

In 1951, the *Indian Act*[4] was revised and section 88 added. Section 88 granted provincial child welfare authorities legal authority on-reserve, and First Nation children began to be apprehended at rates dramatically disproportionate to the population.[5]

The "60's scoop" is a term coined to describe an era in Canadian history between 1960 and the mid-1980s when the highest number of adoptions of Aboriginal children took place. During this time, Aboriginal children were sometimes literally scooped from their homes without knowledge or consent from families or communities. Sometimes buses were hired to remove large numbers of Aboriginal children at a time. Over 11,000 status Indian children, plus many other Aboriginal children, were placed for adoption between 1960 and 1990.[6] These children were adopted by non-Aboriginal families, the result of which was a generation of Aboriginal children raised without cultural knowledge and with confused identities.

COMMUNITY IMPACTS

Cindy Blackstock notes that although though there is enormous diversity among Aboriginal groups in Canada,

> …there are some commonalities that we have found. One is that children were really valued members of the community who brought with them special gifts in the way that they perceive the world and were able to contribute to communities. That it wasn't just the children of this generation or even the generation that followed that were considered in decision making, it was really caring about the generations that communities would never know. So, that whole caring for generations in perpetuity was important.

The important role of Aboriginal children and youth in maintaining healthy Aboriginal communities is inherent in the Aboriginal worldview; their removal to residential schools and by child welfare authorities has been devastating. Nonetheless, the disproportionate removal of Aboriginal children from their homes by child welfare authorities continues to plague Aboriginal communities.

"IN CARE" TODAY

There are currently more Aboriginal children in the care of child welfare authorities than at any point in history; this number continues to rise.[7] Between 1995 and 2001 the number of registered Indian children entering the care of child welfare rose 71.5% nationally.[8]

Aboriginal children are drastically overrepresented in the child welfare system. Blackstock says First Nations Child and Family Caring Society of Canada research from May 2005 indicates that

> . . . in three sample provinces if you were a non-Aboriginal child your chances of going into child welfare care were 0.67%. So that's just one child in every 200 approximately. For Métis children it was 3.31%, so we're up to 6 per 200. And for status Indian children a full 10.23% of them were in child welfare care, which is staggering.

Blackstock concludes,

> We have never in our history had a time when more First Nations kids were in child welfare care than right now, including residential schools and the 60's scoop. If anything we are becoming more efficient at removing kids from their homes.

In addition, despite the interest from Aboriginal families in adoption, a high proportion of Aboriginal children continue to be placed in non-Aboriginal adoptive homes. It is an unfortunate practice to view an Aboriginal child's best interests as being separate from their community and culture. This view is grounded in a focus on the individual, and contrasts with the Aboriginal view of children as a sacred, inextricable part of family, community, and culture.[9] Inevitably, many Aboriginal to non-Aboriginal adoptions break down during adolescence when identity formation is crucial.[10]

BREAKDOWN BY PROVINCE AND TERRITORY

Data about Aboriginal children in care in Canada is not readily available. INAC publishes the number of on-reserve registered status Indian children in care, but finding data about Aboriginal children living in the general population is difficult. Only a few provinces and territories publish regular information about the number of Aboriginal children in care. The National Council of Welfare contacted all provincial and territorial child welfare authorities in 2006 and asked for the total number of Aboriginal and non-Aboriginal children in care. Some readily provided the information, some were reluctant and others were unable or unwilling to do so. Table 7.1 presents the results of this research.

As Table 7.1 indicates, Aboriginal children are grossly overrepresented among children in care. For example, in Manitoba, while 23% of children are Aboriginal (as shown in the first column), 85% of children in care are Aboriginal (as shown in the fourth column). It is difficult to make comparisons between jurisdictions (as described in the text box), but it is clear that there are far more

Table 7.1: Aboriginal children in care by province and territory

	Percent of all children (0-14) who are Aboriginal[11]	Number of children in care			
		Total	Aboriginal	% in care who are Aboriginal	Date
Newfoundland and Labrador	6%				
Prince Edward Island	2%				
Nova Scotia	3%	2,000	310	16%	2006
New Brunswick*	4%	1,445	191	13%	September 30, 2006*
Quebec	2%	11,135			March 31, 2006
Ontario	2%	19,035			March 31, 2006
Manitoba	23%	6,629	5,627	85%	March 31, 2006
Saskatchewan	25%	3,050	2,135	70%	2005
Alberta	9%	8,565	4,880	57%	March 2006
British Columbia	7%	9,157	4,542	50%	March 2006
Yukon**	33%	252			September 2006
Northwest Territories	63%				
Nunavut	95%	311	311	100%	October 2006

* New Brunswick: Data includes 178 First Nations children on-reserve served by First Nations Child and Family Services Agencies as of July 2007.

** Yukon: An estimate from the grand chief of the Council of Yukon First Nations put the share of First Nations children in care at over 80%. (CBC News, "CYFN withdraws from Children's Act review," March 24, 2006.)

Aboriginal children in care than there should be based on population numbers.

Provincial data, where available, shows that the percentage of Aboriginal children in care is increasing. For example, in British Columbia, Aboriginal children made up 37% of children in care in 2000/01, compared to 50% in 2005/06.[12] In 1997 in Manitoba, about 70% of children in care were Aboriginal,[13] compared to 85% at

March 2006. Some of the change is likely due to the growing Aboriginal population, but the increase is too great to be explained away by population growth.

According to National Chief Phil Fontaine, of the Assembly of First Nations (AFN):

The situation facing First Nations children and their families today has never been worse. There are more than 27,000 First Nations children

NO NATIONAL STANDARDS; INADEQUATE NATIONAL FUNDING

There is no national standard for children in care. The provinces and territories have legislative responsibility for child and family services, often called child welfare. Each province and territory has its own legislation that defines how children will be protected from abuse and neglect, and each has different definitions, policies and structures of services. This makes it difficult to compare data from one province or territory to another.

Provincial/territorial child welfare laws apply on reserves, but the federal government retains responsibility under the Indian Act to fund child welfare services provided on-reserve to status Indian children.[14] In February 2007, the Assembly of First Nations and the First Nations Child and Family Caring Society of Canada filed a complaint with the Canadian Human Rights Commission regarding lack of funding for First Nations child welfare.[15]

in care today. This represents three times the number of children who were in residential schools at the height of their operations.[16]

Dr. Cathy Richardson observes that *"on Vancouver Island, 45-50% of the children in care are Aboriginal and one-third of those have quite consistently been Métis."*

Ultimately, many First Nations people would argue that the sixties scoop never ended, it just increased with intensity, each year, each decade. Racism and colonial practices in provincial child welfare systems continue to be challenges for First Nations children and families.[17]

For many generations government policies reflected a belief that European methods of child rearing were superior to First Nation, Inuit, and Métis ways of parenting. The destructive effects of these policies are now readily apparent, yet Aboriginal children continue to be removed

from their families and communities at not only disproportionate, but alarming rates.

CAUSAL FACTORS

"In contrast to other Canadian children, First Nation children are more likely to come into care for neglect rather than sexual abuse, physical abuse, emotional abuse or domestic violence," says Blackstock, *"which is consistent with information from the United States and Australia for their Indigenous populations. In Canada the main factors influencing the removal of a First Nation child for neglect are poverty, poor housing and care giver substance use."*

Blackstock adds,

> *. . . even if a non-Aboriginal family has these same factors, the Aboriginal child is still more*

likely to go into child welfare care. So, race has continued to play a role in child removal.

Dr. Richardson points to the impact of housing on children being taken into care:

We should really create opportunities for different kinds of housing where, for example, instead of removing a child from its parents, we could have a kind of caregiver mentor system where a foster parent came and lived with the young single mom and the children so families could stay together. But we need housing to support those kinds of things.

The AFN stresses the role of poverty in cases of neglect:

The key reason for taking children into care is physical neglect due to poverty...

Only through a comprehensive plan supported by real investments can First Nations finally and forever break free from the prison of poverty.[18]

According to Blackstock there are three key reasons why more First Nations children are in care:

We aren't targeting neglect very well and we're not dealing with structural risk in child welfare to the degree we need to.

Another factor contributing to the over-representation of First Nations children in care relates to the federal government's child welfare funding formula affecting children on reserves. We know that the federal government under-funds child welfare services—particulalry in terms of services intended to build up families so they can safely care for their children. These services are called least disruptive measures. And there's no funding in the federal funding formula for these services, although there is

unlimited money to pull children from their homes.

The third factor is that there is a definite need for reconciliation in child welfare because although people will look retrospectively and say we know better now when you really ask them what they learned from the 60's scoop, what they learned from residential schools and how it has shaped their practice currently, very few people have answers.

And, as noted in other Chapters, the issue of Aboriginal children in care does not stand alone from education, health, employment and other socio-economic indicators and outcomes. According to Blackstock:

There's a study done by Bowlus, McKenna, Day, & Wright (2003) that says the cost of child maltreatment each year costs Canadians a minimum of $16 billion. This is because children who are in child welfare care are more likely to experience health problems as young people and as adults, are less likely to have success in education programs, and therefore in terms of the job market later on, and also are more likely to come to the attention of the criminal justice system. So being in child welfare care is a huge risk. The National Youth in Care Network estimates that a child who's brought into care as a young child will experience as many as 16 moves by the time they are 18.

So, the state makes a lousy parent.

CULTURAL CONTINUITY

Dr. Richardson comments on the role of family violence and cultural dissociation in the overrepresentation of Aboriginal children in care:

There is a lot of violence in the sense that you know women tend to get involved with partners who may need violence as a means of getting what they want and so children sometimes are exposed to violence. It's often violence that leads to involvement in child welfare.

So, one of the things that they've found in terms of helping people heal from a harmful negative experience is an important connection to culture. When we find out that families need help but they are pretty severed from their cultural roots.

So that process of reconnecting with their cultural roots has been a really helpful part of the healing process for people and so that's one of the main mandates of many Métis agencies is to help people sort of rediscover who they are culturally.

And when you find out that somebody might be your kin, or part of your clan, they may be more likely to take you in or help you in times of trouble or take your children. We are trying to encourage that kind of neighborhood-building, community-building in our work.

In the child welfare context, says Blackstock, reconciliation means:

. . . telling the truth about child welfare from multiple perspectives, including non-Indigenous peoples. The other thing that it involves is looking at the values and beliefs that drove us to do certain things. Part of the reason we don't learn is that we don't look underneath our actions to understand how it helped us rationalize bad outcomes when they were in front of us.

The second part of it is that once we have heard the truths we need to acknowledge that non-Aboriginal child welfare has been around for

about 100 years and the diverse Indigenous communities in Canada have been practicing various forms of child welfare going back for about 20,000 years. So, child welfare on the basis of time in terms of practice needs to be humble in what it knows. It needs to set aside the arrogance that we know what's best for you and embrace other ways of knowing and looking at the world in terms of Indigenous children.

It also means understanding that the current system is not working and is culturally loaded. People assume that the current child welfare system is culturally neutral but it's only neutral to the British and the French because it's based on that worldview. So, it's not surprising that Aboriginal people and new Canadians are the least well served by the child welfare system.

The third phase of this is about restoring. That's about saying, we need to provide an opportunity to those who have done harm in the past to try and redress those harms that are possible to redress, and to put in place plans to prevent its recurrence. We need to find ways of awakening each other to the contemporary manifestations of racism, and putting in place really pragmatic meaningful ways of guarding against it.

The fourth phase is relating and that is to understand that reconciliation is not an event, it's a long term commitment to working together.

While there are no quick fixes to the child welfare system and its interaction with Aboriginal children, there are nonetheless approaches including government-to-government ones, that work in the spirit of reconciliation and restoration.

ABORIGINAL CARE OF ABORIGINAL CHILDREN

First Nations, Inuit, and Métis peoples have practiced effective ways of raising, caring for, and protecting their children throughout their history.[19] The failure of provincial/territorial child welfare agencies to make a meaningful difference in the health and well being of Aboriginal children supports the need for Aboriginal controlled, culturally based models.

For Dr. Richardson, the cultural connection often proves fundamental in keeping Métis children out of care:

> So one of the programs that have been particularly helpful here has been the Root program. That has been sponsored by NCSV Native Community Services of Victoria. We take children from care and try to find family. We also have a volunteer genealogist who helps us support that work. Many of the children in care don't know their families in the Prairies or other places. So this program has been very successful but it could be even more successful in reuniting families that have been separated for various historical reasons.

Respect for culture combined with Aboriginal control over child Aboriginal welfare appears to be on the "right track". According to Dr. Richardson,

> I've heard a lot of positive talk and of course in British Columbia there has been a movement towards creating what they call "delegated Aboriginal child welfare agencies" and there are different levels of delegation. Some of those kinds of agencies exist and I think it is definitely the right track to go along. It has all been treaty processes encouraging Aboriginal community capacity-building and the kind of things that would support those kinds of programs. We need to do a lot of work around safety.

> So I think the ideas around family-conferencing and these sorts of justice programs are certainly the right step but I think we still need to shift our paradigm of working from one where we tell other people what to do to one where we bring families together and listen to them and ask them, "What kind of support do you need?" "How can we help you to take care of your children and keep them safe?" I think if we did that or just gave a lot of the money to community and put offers to create partnerships and put things in place to create or monitor safety of children that might be a better use of resources.

> But it's also about handing the programs to the people who could run it efficiently. When we see programs moving to delegated Aboriginal agencies, what has happened is that the government wants to offer about half the money to deliver the service that it is currently delivering. It isn't always feasible and I do think maybe communities could deliver services for somewhat less money if you get rid of the middle people and the bureaucratic element. But I don't think you can expect these positive changes to come anytime quickly. I think it's an ongoing process. We have to keep moving in that direction. But at the same time we have to really keep a critical eye on all of our agencies, both mainstream and Aboriginal. What are they doing to protect women and children and victims, vulnerable people, from violence?

Blackstock also has a vision for addressing Aboriginal child welfare:

We have developed something called Reconciliation in Child Welfare: Touchstones of Hope for Indigenous Children, Youth, and Families. Basically what the five principles are is self-determination, culture and language, holistic approach, structural intervention, and non-discrimination.

One of the things we would encourage Canada to do is to stop rolling out preformed solutions and instead, fund communities to develop their own solutions based on the touchstone principles. These principles are constitutional in nature in that they are to be interpreted at a local community level allowing for unique cultural, linguistic and contextual differences. So, for example, culture and language would look very different in a Cree community than it would in a Mi'kmaw community in Nova Scotia. Those would be interpreted locally but it would still allow a national framework that really speaks to what is important for the well being of Indigenous children.

The other thing that we think is strongly needed is funding. Canada will fund national programs, but they never fund First Nation, Inuit, or Métis communities to develop community development plans that put children and youth at the centre, so that that community can dream what is important for them in their context. Canada can provide resources to meet those needs, instead of providing these resources on a national roll-out basis, which is often irrelevant to the needs of many communities.

Blackstock adds,

The current reality is that First Nations child and family service agencies must operate pursuant to provincial child welfare laws, unless your First Nation has a self-government agreement that specifically includes child welfare, you must operate under provincial legislation. There is only one emerging example where First Nations have been around the drafting table of child welfare legislation, and that is in Manitoba. In other regions it is primarily the province on its own which will draft this legislation regardless of the disproportionate rate of Aboriginal children in care.

Indigenous people are in the best position to make decisions about Indigenous children. And there still is a lot of paternalism in the child welfare system, in the way it is administered. These principles are meant to re-shape that to really ensure that at all levels this truly is a partnership where Indigenous peoples are taking the lead in Indigenous care programs for Indigenous children. So, Manitoba has worked with First Nations and Métis communities to develop the Aboriginal Justice Inquiry-Child Welfare Initiative. That is definitely the most progressive model in the country.

It's critical that First Nations administer their own child welfare systems. There's good research that says the best outcomes for Indigenous children come when Indigenous communities have the decision making authority, and they have the resources to implement it. Yet, having that decision making authority also means having decision making responsibility. In contrast to western child welfare systems that empower professionals to deal with things that are painful in communities, in our traditional systems everyone was held accountable when a child was abused. Unless we link community development and community responsibility we won't have children living in the types of situations we want them to live in.

In order for communities to run these programs effectively Blackstock says,

They need to have their own authority recognized. They need to be empowered with the opportunity to dream. Canada does not have to come up with solutions. It spends way too much time doing that. Communities already have the solutions. They need to be given the opportunity for the whole community to generate what makes sense to them, and then to have that adequately and sustainably resourced without all the strings attached through the funding mechanisms from Canada. Because Canada will sometimes say broadly that it supports a certain outcome, and yes we will allow First Nations communities to deliver the program in whatever way but through the funding mechanisms they really drive and restrict that process.

Inherent in greater Aboriginal community ownership of child welfare is a fundamental rethinking of the mainstream colonial approach to Aboriginal children in which the dominant culture perceives that it knows best.

For Dr. Richardson,

The education of social workers has become so important to me because I think rather inadvertently the government is still the government and there is still a colonial mentality at work there.

I think one of the basic aspects of the colonial framework is this sort of three-part message. One is "I am proficient" and that is "I am the model. I am a European

Canadian. I am proud to be part of the mainstream. This is how we do things and we like people to act like us when they come to Canada." And, "So you should be like us. And if you're not like us. . . "

The second part of the message is that "you are deficient because you are different."

And the third part of the message is, "therefore, I have the right to do what I want to you in order to help you, or fix you, or to make life better for you." So that can be "I'm going to diagnose you, I'm going to put you in Ministry care," whatever it is.

Dr. Cathy Richardson

We have found that due to this kind of mentality, rather than supporting families, historically the Ministry has taken children into foster care and as a result many children today, even adults, are facing the many abuses that they suffered in foster care.

Structural reasons why Aboriginal children are being taken into care must also be dealt with, including poverty, lack of education, unemployment, housing and myriad other interconnected factors.

Dr. Richardson describes the treatment of Aboriginal children in care as being the next human rights violation in Canada, while Blackstock concludes:

> *They will look back at people like you and I and they will say did you know that so many First Nations kids were in child welfare care? And we did. And were there solutions? And there were. And what did we do about implementing them?*
>
> *That's the chapter that we are going to be writing over the next year as Canadians. Our history in the past, in residential schools and in the 60's Scoop, is that we stood still. So, we have a chance to make that right by making sure that we are not standing still and silent this time.*

IN SUMMARY

Aboriginal children and youth are an intrinsic component of healthy Aboriginal communities; their removal to residential schools and by child welfare authorities has been devastating. Nonetheless, the disproportionate removal of Aboriginal children from their homes by child welfare authorities continues.

Aboriginal peoples are best positioned to make decisions about Aboriginal children and youth. In the spirit of reconciliation and restoration, there is a need for adequately funded, Aboriginal controlled, culturally based models of childcare while also tackling the myriad interconnected factors such as poverty that facilitate Aboriginal children ending up in care.

CHAPTER 8

JUSTICE
AND
ABORIGINAL YOUTH

I think current wellness does relate to the history and I think that it hasn't helped that a lot of it has really been silenced and made invisible. So for example, if you've seen the Royal Commission on Aboriginal People "No Turning Back" film, when the Commissioners go to a prison and are talking to a group of Aboriginal people, they say "How many of you share this man's experiences where you were in a foster home and you were abused by the people who had the responsibility of looking after you?" Almost everyone in the room put up their hand.

Dr. Cathy Richardson

Aboriginal peoples are vastly over-represented in the Canadian penal system, federal and provincial, arising from a myriad of factors including systemic racism, disadvantage in Canadian society and a mainstream justice system that is not reflective of Aboriginal justice, thereby rendering it ineffective for these offenders. Many Aboriginal children "graduate" from being children in care to being youth and adults in the criminal justice system. Legislation and program funding have facilitated some renewal in traditional Aboriginal justice including sentencing circles and community restorative justice initiatives, though this approach is not without its critics.

OVER-REPRESENTATION
OF ABORIGINAL PEOPLE

Canada has an overall incarceration rate of 130 per 100,000 adults, including both provincial and federal institutions. The estimated incarceration rate for Aboriginal people in Canada is 1,024 per 100,000 adults and for non-Aboriginal persons it is 117 per 100,000 adults.[1] Aboriginal people are almost nine times more likely to be locked up than non-Aboriginal people.

Perhaps even more startling is that

while the federally incarcerated population in Canada declined by 12.5% from 1996 to 2004, the number of First Nations people in federal institutions increased by 21.7%. The number of incarcerated First Nations women also increased—by 74.2% over the same period.[2]

If the current trend continues unchecked, the "Aboriginal population in Canada's correctional institutions could reach the 25% mark in less than 10 years." [3]

In its 2005-2006 annual report, the Office of the Correctional Investigator of Canada condemned ongoing discrimination against Aboriginal people in the justice system.

> Despite some positive steps, the overall situation of Aboriginal offenders has not measurably improved in recent years. Aboriginals account for a disproportionate share of the prison population. They represent 18% of the federal prison population although they account for just 3% of the general Canadian population.[4]

The Correctional Investigator noted,

> The higher rate of recidivism for Aboriginal offenders is in part due to the Correctional Service's failure to manage Aboriginal inmates in a culturally responsive and non-discriminatory manner.[5]

A recent study for the federal Department of Justice observes:

> Aboriginal peoples experience systemic discrimination every time they come into contact with the justice system. Systemic discrimination is the norm and affects offenders and victims indiscriminately. It is pervasive and endemic.[6]

Despite dozens of past reports detailing similar findings, including the National

Council of Welfare's *Justice and the Poor*,[7] little has changed, with Aboriginal youth disproportionately admitted to remand and sentenced to custody.

ABORIGINAL YOUTH: OFFENDERS AND VICTIMS

As Offenders

The proportion of Aboriginal youth admitted to remand and sentenced custody declined between 1998/1999 and 2002/2003 but rose again in 2003/2004, the first year following the implementation of the *Youth Criminal Justice Act*. At the same time, the number of Aboriginal youth sentenced to custody dropped by 33% from 2002/2003 to 2003/2004 while non-Aboriginal youth admissions declined by 51%. Aboriginal youth admissions to remand went up by 3% while non-Aboriginal youth declined by 17%.[8]

In 2000, 41.3 % of all federally incarcerated Aboriginal offenders were 25 years of age or younger.[9]

The situation of Aboriginal young people in regards to the justice system is harsh, as shown in Table 8.1:

Table 8.1: Aboriginal Young Persons Admitted to Correctional Services, 2003/04					
		Sentenced Custody			
Jurisdiction	Remand	Open Custody	Secure Custody	Probation	Aboriginal youth as % of total youth population
	% of young persons who are Aboriginal				
TOTAL	**27%**	**30%**	**27%**	**17%**	**5%**
Newfoundland and Labrador	3%	9%	8%	4%	5%
Prince Edward Island	...	...	...	...	1%
Nova Scotia	6%	8%	0%	6%	3%
New Brunswick	5%	4%	7%	8%	3%
Quebec	...	...	...	...	2%
Ontario - 12 to 15 years old	...	6%	1%	3%	2%
- 16 to 17 years old	11%	10%	16%	8%	2%
Manitoba	71%	82%	77%	56%	19%
Saskatchewan	...	84%	75%	65%	19%
Alberta	39%	44%	37%	29%	8%
British Columbia	36%	35%	32%	29%	7%
Yukon	91%	100%	...	83%	26%
Northwest Territories	88%	100%	83%	...	63%
Nunavut	100%	100%	100%	...	95%

...	not available

Source: Donna Calverly, Youth Custody and Community Services in Canada, 2003/04

While Aboriginal youth form 5% of the youth population, across Canada they constitute:

- 27% of those on remand;
- 30% of those in open custody;
- 27% of those in secure custody; and
- 17% of those on probation.

In the four western provinces, the numbers reach astronomic proportions; for example, in Manitoba 77% of youth in secure custody are Aboriginal, in Saskatchewan Aboriginal youth are 75%, in Alberta 37% and 32% in British Columbia. Given that Aboriginal youth form 19% of the population in Saskatchewan and Manitoba, 8% in Alberta and 7% in B.C., the percentages in secure custody are far out of balance with population numbers, as they are for all other types of admittance to correctional services.

A one day snapshot of the justice system carried out in 2004 established that

> the incarceration rate of Aboriginal youth was 64.5 per 10,000 population while the incarceration rate for non-Aboriginal youth was 8.2 per 10,000 population. Aboriginal youth were almost eight times more likely to be in custody compared to their non-Aboriginal counterparts.[10]

A study of the origins of the Aboriginal youth in custody indicated some 78% are of First Nations origin compared to 16% who were Métis and 3% Inuit.[11]

Aboriginal young offenders also spend, on average, longer periods in custody than non-Aboriginal young offenders for the same offences. However, this finding should be viewed with caution as it does not take into account the criminal history of the youth and the seriousness of the offence.[12]

As Victims

Aboriginal people are three times more likely than non-Aboriginal people to experience a violent victimization (319 versus 101 incidents per 1,000 population). Younger Aboriginal people aged 15-34 years of age were 2.5 times more likely to be victims of violent crime as those who were 35 years and older (461 incidents versus 192 incidents per 1,000 population).[13]

Aboriginal young women are disproportionately victimized in domestic violence, the sex trade, and gang violence.[14] Young Aboriginal women are subject to gendered racism and violence targeted at Aboriginal women in general, and more particularly, as sex trade workers. The justice system has often been slow to react as witnessed by the incredible numbers of missing Aboriginal young women (over 500) in many cities.[15]

Initiatives, such as Sisters in Spirit, provide a promising example of collaborative efforts. In this initiative, the Native Women's Association of Canada (NWAC) is working in collaboration with Aboriginal youth, other Aboriginal women's organizations and the federal government to address the high rates of missing and murdered Aboriginal women in Canada. As noted by NWAC, "this type of violence typically occurs in the public sphere, where societal indifference often leaves Aboriginal women at greater risk." Accordingly, this five-year research, education and policy initiative is designed to increase public understanding and knowledge of the impact of racialized and sexualized violence against Aboriginal women often leading to their disappearance and death.[16]

CAUSAL FACTORS:
500 YEARS IN THE MAKING

As our interview with Justice Murray Sinclair indicates, the over representation of Aboriginal youth in the justice system was 500 years in the making. Colonization, racism, loss of land, and disempowerment are the root causes of poverty which in turn impacts Aboriginal youth in the justice system. Compared to non-Aboriginal youth, Aboriginal youth have limited access to education and recreational facilities and fewer employment opportunities.

The RCAP report notes:

> [M]any factors contribute to weakening the fabric of a society and loosening the bonds of relationships and self-regulated behavior: social change that is rapid or beyond the control of a society; family breakdown, which interferes with the nurturing and socialization of children; poverty and economic marginalization, which restrict opportunities for youth and contribute to a loss of hope; loss of respect for the wisdom of Aboriginal people's culture; and learned patterns of self-defeating or self-destructive behavior passed on from one generation to another. . .

> In our hearings and commissioned research we found further evidence that assaults on Aboriginal identity, culture and community institutions continue today. Aboriginal people recounted racially motivated incidents experienced in their daily lives. The stereotyping and devaluing of Aboriginal women, a combination of racism and sexism, are among the most damaging of attitudes that find expression in Canadian society. These attitudes are not held exclusively by non-Aboriginal people either. Indeed . . . members of powerless groups who are subjected to demeaning treatment tend to internalize negative attitudes toward their own group. They then act on those attitudes in ways that confirm the original negative judgment." [17]

A Canadian Criminal Justice Association report noted the extra stress placed on Aboriginal youth: "They [Aboriginal youth] must try to adapt to mainstream Canadian society while at the same time attempting to learn and retain their traditional culture." [18]

The one day snapshot portrait developed at length the link between poor social and economic conditions and high rates of custody:

- 47% of Aboriginal youth in custody came from families on social assistance;

- 39% of Aboriginal youth in custody were involved with child protection agencies at the time of their admission—of these youth, one in four was a ward of the state;

- Grade eight was the highest average grade completed by Aboriginal youth at the time of their admission to custody;

- Only 2% of Aboriginal youth in custody aged 18 and over had successfully completed high school;

- 57% of Aboriginal youth had a confirmed drug problem;

- Another 24% had a suspected problem with substance abuse; and

- About one in six Aboriginal youth in custody was "suspected or confirmed to have had Fetal Alcohol Spectrum Disorder (FASD)—4% reported a confirmed medical diagnosis, 5% were suspected by the custody facility, and 8% self-reported that they had FASD." [19]

> *The justice system generally doesn't deal with social conditions very well. By that I mean that the vast majority of Aboriginal youth that get caught up in the justice system are kids who are troubled with issues surrounding self-esteem, poverty, family dysfunction and even social rejection and the result is that they get caught up in social activities and social groups that put them in conflict with the law, that put them in conflict with institutions and generally put them in a position where they are unable to take advantage of either the resources that are available in society generally, or of the basic legal processes that anybody who comes into trouble with the law has access to.*
>
> Justice Murray Sinclair

According to Justice Sinclair, somewhat different issues are faced by urban and reserve Aboriginal populations:

> *I think there's generally a difference between the urban Aboriginal population and the reserve population and it has to do with, and this is an overly-broad generalization I recognize, but I would say for the most part the urban Aboriginal population consists of people who have chosen to be in an urban environment. Sometimes the choice has been imposed upon them in the sense that in order to go to school or go to university they have to move to an urban area, but at the same time they make the choice of going to that institution or taking advantage of that activity or whatever it might be, knowing that it is going to put them in an urban environment.*
>
> *Having said that, I would say that to a large extent I suspect and I haven't looked at the numbers, or the last two sets of Stats Can data, I believe the urban Aboriginal population has a much higher income than the reserve population. There's a higher level of education. There's a higher level of employment and generally a higher living standard among the urban Aboriginal population. I would say probably that is true, certainly that's true in Manitoba. That is probably true across Canada.*
>
> *We know that for the most part, again there are exceptions to this: reserve populations are generally in more isolated areas of the province where employment is not as good. There is a higher level of unemployment and as a result a higher level of dependency on social assistance programs, less ability to have and develop a career. So as a result of that I think there are differences between the two populations. But in addition, I think as well, the urban population probably feels more disconnected to its traditional roots to its history, to its culture, to the language and so those also cause, I think, a different set of issues or problems for the urban population that may not be as strong in the reserve communities.*
>
> *Having said that, I know that reserve communities would say it is because of the urban influence—because of the gang environment for example—which is reaching back into the reserves as a client base for drug dealing. Youth in Aboriginal communities are also becoming more disconnected to history and the culture and traditions. We know, for example, I think it's fair to say in Manitoba, that*

virtually all of the drug trade in First Nations communities in Manitoba is controlled by urban Aboriginal gangs. And I think that is probably true not only in Manitoba but also in the Prairie provinces and generally throughout Canada. So there is that influence and that connection.

With respect to the Métis community says Justice Sinclair,

The disparity in the resources available to First Nations people vs. the resources available to Métis communities who are often in the very same social situations is amazing and that also needs to be addressed.

If you go to any First Nations community in Manitoba and I think this is probably true in Ontario and Saskatchewan, there is a Métis community living right beside it, living across the road and the social conditions are the same, the living conditions are the same but the resources available to one vs. the resources available to the other are different. That often results in conflict within the community; sometimes conflict within families, particularly given the continuing disenfranchisement from the Indian Act that says that people lose status because of who they marry.

In addition to that, they don't have the same level of self-determination. The same level of self-government or self-control over issues and decision-making within the community. There are those things that need to be addressed.

Dr. Richardson adds,

Of course our Métis numbers are highly represented in various institutions. In child welfare. In prisons. But we are under-represented in institutions of higher learning, wealthier neighborhoods and those

kinds of things although you will find Métis all across the economic spectrum.

Parliament recognized the overrepresentation of Aboriginal offenders in corrections and some of the root causes, in enacting subsection 718.2(e) of the *Criminal Code* in 1996.[20] This provision and section 50 of the *Youth Criminal Justice Act* of 2002,[21] mandate judges to take a more culturally relevant, contextual approach to sentencing Aboriginal offenders.

RESTORATIVE APPROACHES/ ALTERNATIVE MEASURES

There is no quick fix within the justice system to address the situation of Aboriginal youth. However this does not mean that alternate approaches to the mainstream justice system should not be implemented and advanced. Aboriginal alternatives to the mainstream justice system have sprung up because of its failure to provide healing, rehabilitation and restoration among other factors.

In recent years, alternative measures have been encouraged as a result of the reform of the *Criminal Code* and the new *Youth Criminal Justice Act*. Subsection 718.2(e) of the *Criminal Code* currently requires that a court consider all available sanctions other than imprisonment that are reasonable in the circumstances, with particular attention to the circumstances of Aboriginal offenders. Section 50 of the *Youth Criminal Justice Act* provides that subsection 718.2(e) applies to young offenders.

Alternative measures include pre- and post-charge diversion, alternative sentencing including sentencing circles, and community based conditional sentencing.

While some 9,800 First Nations young people were accused of a criminal offence on-reserve, 44% were formally charged and the rest cleared[22] by alternate measures, which is identical to the percentages of youth at large dealt with in this manner.[23] Alternate measures could include formal measures such as a Crown caution or extrajudicial sanctions, or informal measures such as a police warning or referral to a community program.[24]

According to Justice Sinclair,

> At the time that I graduated from law school in 1979, the number of Aboriginal youth caught up in the justice system was disproportionately high and continues to be and probably if there has been a change it has been that that disproportion has increased so that we are now seeing a higher proportion of Aboriginal youth incarcerated and charged in the justice system. I think the latest increases in the last five or six years, particularly since the Youth Criminal Justice Act, in my view, has been because the benefits of the Youth Criminal Justice Act have largely weighed in favour of those who can take advantage of the intent of the legislation and that has not been Aboriginal youth.

> I would say overall there has been a benefit to youth at large. I think the gross numbers of youth being diverted is probably greater. The gross numbers of youth who are charged is probably lower and the gross number of youth who are incarcerated probably lower. I know from observation and from the reports from people who are working in the youth correctional system that the actual number of bodies of youth who are being incarcerated is lower. But the proportion of Aboriginal youth has actually increased because the number of non-Aboriginal youth who are being diverted and who are not being incarcerated has increased disproportionately from what they were in previous years. Whereas I don't think the proportion of Aboriginal youth who have taken advantage of the intent of the legislation has increased in the same way.

> I would guess it's because the ongoing impact of discretion within the justice system is still significant and all of the studies have shown that when discretion is exercised to the benefit of a youth by either police officers or prosecutors, generally it is exercised more likely in favour of those who are representative of the social class or status and background of the discretion-holder: the police officer or the prosecutor. So that's generally the white, middle-class kids because the police officer or the decision-maker within the police force or the prosecutor is more-inclined to exercise discretion in terms of youth with whom he or she most closely identifies from a social background. So there's that element at work and that's always been at play.

> Secondly, though, I think with the intent behind the Youth Criminal Justice Act to call upon the resources within the community and for youth to be diverted to existing resources in the community, when it comes to Aboriginal youth there's not that many resources that are specifically focused upon them.

Thus, alternative measures should go hand in hand with funding for broader community justice initiatives as well as major anti-racism reform of the criminal justice system, including police, prosecutors and judges. Indeed, RCAP concluded that "systemic discrimination contributes to Aboriginal victimization because the existing system does not address, and is inherently incapable of addressing, the underlying causes of Aboriginal criminality."

However, it is important to note that issues have also been raised by Aboriginal women pertaining to restorative justice sentencing for male offenders convicted of crimes involving violence and abuse, and whether their victims (often Aboriginal women) have adequate voice.

Dr. Richardson, while supportive of delegating justice programs to Aboriginal agencies, observes:

> But at the same time we have to really keep a critical eye on all of our agencies, both mainstream and Aboriginal. What are they doing to protect women and children and victims, vulnerable people from violence? It's an ongoing problem everywhere. So I worry about the alternate dispute resolution processes and circle sentencing for cases that involve violence against people. Because I don't think that we have yet accountability and enough safety in communities to really deal with the needs of victims, before, during and after the processes.
>
> Agencies need to be a part of it, and the police, and groups that help children, youth and women. There needs to be really cohesive networks to make sure that people are going to be safe. At this point I think even though there are safe people in every family there are also skyrocketing levels of violence in many communities and I think this move to alternative justice means that the mainstream justice system hasn't worked properly.

> So I'm worried about unleashing a lot of things on the community when there really isn't enough to really keep people safe. Children are very vulnerable and they need adults to take care of them. I think the process of community development and Aboriginal sovereignty and all those things have to move ahead side-by-side by paying attention to safety.

Thus Aboriginal justice must be approached from a holistic, "justice writ large" perspective, recognizing that not only are Aboriginal people disproportionately criminalized but also disproportionately victimized.

HOLISTIC APPROACHES: JUSTICE WRIT LARGE

Aboriginal youth face race and gender discrimination, often further compounded by inequity due to poverty, ill-health, lack of education and employment opportunities and other factors.

This discrimination is evidenced within the justice system by disproportionate rates of charging, prosecution and conviction of Aboriginal people and their over-representation in prisons.

Justice system options include increasing Aboriginal people's access to legal aid, cultural awareness training for police, prosecutors, judges and corrections staff, and the recruitment of more Aboriginal people throughout the justice system. Aboriginal people also need access to culturally appropriate life skills programs and community re-integration supports. Traditional

Aboriginal justice initiatives may also deliver more culturally meaningful justice to Aboriginal youth and communities while providing greater potential for rehabilitation.

However, in order to effectively implement such programs, governments must cease the inter-jurisdictional wrangling and buck-passing that hinders progress. As noted by Justice Sinclair,

> *Probably the first area that requires resolution, and I think everybody who has worked in this area knows it, is that the whole federal/provincial conflict over jurisdiction of First Nations people needs to be resolved. Particularly for the urban Aboriginal population because there is a strong desire by Aboriginal people to maintain, even urban Aboriginal people, First Nations people, to maintain a connection to their community and to receive services from their community-based institutions, such as child welfare and education. And yet the Federal government denies coverage or services or rights to that population. So the urban Aboriginal, urban First Nations person is left to compete with the rest of the urban populations for the limited resources that the province supplies to the urban community.*

> *The Federal government claims that they are only responsible for Aboriginal people who are actually residing in First Nations areas and I think most legal advisors say that's not correct. But that conflict has not been resolved and until it is there's always going to be that tension and as a result there are going to be*

> *Aboriginal First Nations people who fall through the cracks.*

While alternative approaches to a criminal justice system that is clearly not working for Aboriginal peoples are to be lauded, truly addressing Aboriginal over-representation requires a holistic approach.

According to Justice Sinclair,

> *The overall solution, I think, is going to be a long term approach and it has to begin with early childhood development issues. There, I think, we need to assist, particularly given the higher birth rates and the number of young Aboriginal girls who are getting pregnant and having babies before the age of 20. We have to assist them to develop their parenting skills and their own personal levels of achievement so that they themselves can be good role models for their children as they are growing up, as well as good contributing members of society, be that an Aboriginal community or the overall community.*

> *I think there has been a recognition in Canada of the importance of early childhood development programs and early childhood nurturing issues and even addressing issues in the fetal development stage. I think we just need to ensure that those programs are focused heavily towards those who have the least ability to take advantage of them in Canada or which at least in Manitoba is the Aboriginal community.*

> *We have to look at pinpointing and focusing our efforts. Certainly the efforts need to be directed at youth because*

in the long run the youth are going to become the people of the future. Recognize the growing population of Aboriginal people and the fact that as they grow older there is going to be more demand made upon the system by them.

I think it is young people who are going to benefit in the long run from our attention so we should be focusing our resources on early childhood issues. Early childhood development centres in urban areas, for example. I think we should have parenting centres available to young Aboriginal parents, mothers in particular because we know that most of the Aboriginal children who are being born in urban environments are being born into single-parent situations.

Now mind you, this single-parent often has her parents, grandparents available to assist her in the raising of a child. That type of a family dynamic doesn't mean that the mother is able to cope with the demands made upon her as a mother. And I think that is what she needs help with. Even simple things like putting in a daycare centre in a school that has a large Aboriginal population makes a lot of sense to me and yet the school divisions are not addressing that.

I think we also need to look at identifying the young Aboriginal parents and assisting them to develop their skills through connecting them to grandmothers and grandfathers who are prepared to help them as parents. Because of the history of Aboriginal, particularly First Nations and also Métis in this province, we often have Aboriginal families in an urban setting who don't

have access to grandparents, access to elders in their family to assist them whether it is decision-making or simple skill development. Having grandparent centres where young Aboriginal people could benefit from meeting with grandparents who have experience and can just help them and support them, I think is a worthwhile endeavor.

Ultimately, the real solutions also lay in tackling oppression, racism and discrimination, and in the political and economic empowerment of Aboriginal peoples. Adds Justice Sinclair,

My view is this is a long-standing and long-developing problem that we are now coming face-to-face with. The result is that we are now seeing the results of a hundred years of oppression or more—colonialism that no other group in society has ever experienced. Because of that, no other group in society has yet been able to develop solutions to deal with it adequately, having regard to the interests of Aboriginal people to maintain their culture, their traditions, their community, as well as their unique rights.

This means developing a series of new strategies and measures designed by and for Aboriginal peoples. This will require commitment from all levels of government and fortitude. Ultimately, says Justice Sinclair,

I keep telling people that it has taken us 500 years to get to this point, we're not going to get out of it in 500 years. It's a lot easier to knock something down than it is to build it.

IN SUMMARY

Aboriginal youth face discrimination, inequity due to poverty, ill-health, lack of education and employment opportunities and other factors. This is evidenced within the justice system by disproportionate rates of charging, prosecution and conviction of Aboriginal people and their over-representation in prisons. It is also seen in the high proportion of Aboriginal women who are victims of racialized and sexualized violence.

There are numerous approaches that may reduce this disproportionate representation, including culturally appropriate justice initiatives; however, the needs of victims and the concerns of Aboriginal women must be addressed in their development. Effective implementation also requires an end to governmental inter-jurisdictional wrangling.

A focus on early years programming for Aboriginal children and their parents is a front-end preventative approach that also shows promise. Truly addressing Aboriginal over-representation requires a holistic approach to tackle oppression, racism and discrimination, and to foster the political and economic empowerment of Aboriginal peoples.

FINAL THOUGHTS AND RECOMMENDATIONS

We hope the statistics and interviews in this report have helped readers reflect carefully on what it means to grow up Aboriginal in Canada. First Nations, Métis and Inuit children and youth, along with adults upon whom they depend, face enormous current and historical barriers.

Yet there are Aboriginal women, men, children and young people who are succeeding against the odds, offering help and hope to others. The young Aboriginal population is growing and that offers an unparalleled opportunity for a country facing population ageing and a shrinking labour force. But, simply put, the rest of us have to care about Aboriginal well-being. We have to build a more inclusive society where Aboriginal people can benefit. If we do not, an increasing rate of human misery—and militancy—is almost certainly to be expected. This doesn't serve anyone well.

The National Council of Welfare is not an Aboriginal organization but it has a unique mandate to advise the federal government on poverty and social development. From this perspective, we are making what we believe are important recommendations. We are not experts on First Nations, Métis and Inuit issues, and our goal is to support and complement the recommendations already made in RCAP and beyond by Aboriginal organizations.

Indeed, we have three main goals in writing this report.

- First, we see it as a way of adding our voice to support Aboriginal peoples in their demands for government action to fight poverty and exclusion and to create opportunities for a better future.

- Second, we hope it will enlighten non-Aboriginal readers so they too can be more supportive of the bold and holistic change that is needed.

- Third, we want to convey our own impatience and urgency to the federal government; it is immoral that government after government has made so many harmful decisions, broken so many promises and left so many Aboriginal people in destitution and despair. Yet the federal government has the means and opportunity to turn that pattern around, if it has the will.

Canada is a rich country. Collectively, we have choices—far more choices than most Aboriginal children and youth can even imagine.

THE NCW ENCOURAGES CANADIANS TO CHOOSE TO:

1) Build understanding and support for Aboriginal peoples in whatever way we can and in ways that First Nations, Métis and Inuit individuals or organizations want. For example, we could read and learn more, listen to individual Aboriginal life stories, participate in Aboriginal cultural and political events, work with individuals and organizations in our communities. We can also show our support to local media, through letters to newspaper editors or radio talk shows.

2) Take a stand against racism when we see it occur. We can challenge assumptions we and others may have about Aboriginal people in our schools, workplaces and neighbourhoods.

3) Make sure our municipal, provincial, territorial and federal government representatives know that we support action to improve Aboriginal lives.

THE NCW WANTS THE FEDERAL, AND OTHER, GOVERNMENTS TO CHOOSE TO:

1) Adopt a national anti-poverty strategy, as outlined in the NCW's *Solving Poverty: Four Cornerstones of a Workable National Strategy for Canada*. Aboriginal poverty cannot be solved in isolation from other Canadians who are also impoverished due to factors like disability, racism, sexism and lone-parenthood. And as highlighted repeatedly in this report, challenges facing Aboriginal people cannot be solved in isolation; everything is interconnected. The only way forward is a comprehensive strategy.

2) Adopt, within this national strategy, a specific long-term vision for Aboriginal peoples along with targets, timelines, indicators, intergovernmental coordination, and accountability to Aboriginal Canadians for results.

3) Include First Nations, Métis and Inuit people in creating every part of the strategy, and guarantee that women have an equal say, especially in the interests of children, and that young women and men and girls and boys themselves will also have their voices heard.

4) Immediately invest sufficient resources to meet the basic needs of every Aboriginal child and young person, regardless of their status or where they live (food, clothing, drinkable water, safe housing, early learning and care, access to education and health care) through increased income and services that foster autonomy and dignity.

5) Immediately invest much more heavily in programs and policies that are working for children and youth or show promise—there are numerous examples in this report of what works, largely because Aboriginal people design and run them to meet needs that they understand. But the need in every case outstrips the capacity. With greater funding and other supports, they can be continued, expanded, replicated in other places and adapted to other needs to greatly advance the achievement of healing, human development and societal reconstruction.

6) Speed up and work harder, in good faith, to build fair, sustainable governance frameworks for all Aboriginal peoples to render the *Indian Act* and the colonial, paternalistic power relations it represents null and void. First Nations, Métis, Inuit and non-Aboriginal Canadians have all been affected in different ways by the poisonous relationships the Act has created.

7) Set aside federal, provincial, territorial, and municipal government wrangling and work together, along with Aboriginal governments and organizations, to get lasting results.

8) Start by adopting comprehensive negotiated agreements with Aboriginal peoples and by speeding up the process of settling land claims. Then continue to build a larger framework that enables all Aboriginal women, men and children to attain a decent quality of life.

Poverty is a political choice. Social inclusion and well-being are equally possible. There are no excuses in this country to give in to the status quo.

INTRODUCTION

1   Unfortunately, the information available and collected does not always represent the full diversity of Aboriginal peoples.

2   See, for example, Congress of Aboriginal Peoples, *Background Paper for the Accountability for Results Round Table, January 25&26, 2005: A Proposed Solution* (Ottawa: Congress of Aboriginal Peoples, 2005) http://www.aboriginalroundtable.com/sect/acnt/bckpr/CAP_BgPaper_e.pdf and Statistics Canada, "Aboriginal Peoples of Canada: Definitions" (Ottawa: Statistics Canada, [n.d]), accessed August 23, 2007. http://www12.statcan.ca/english/census01/Products/Analytic/companion/abor/definitions.cfm

3   For more extensive information on the history and perspectives of different Aboriginal peoples see, for example, Canada, Royal Commission on Aboriginal Peoples, Report of the Royal Commission on Aboriginal Peoples, 5 vols. (Ottawa: Minister of Supply and Services, 1996). http://www.ainc-inac.gc.ca/ch/rcap/

4   *Constitution Act, 1867*, s. 91(24).

5   Canada, Royal Commission on Aboriginal Peoples, *Highlights from the Report of the Royal Commission on Aboriginal Peoples,* (Ottawa: Minister of Supply and Services, 1996). http://www.ainc-inac.gc.ca/ch/rcap/rpt/lk_e.html

6   Assembly of First Nations, *Royal Commission on Aboriginal People at 10 Years: A Report Card* (Ottawa: AFN, 2006). http://www.afn.ca/cmslib/general/afn_rcap.pdf

7   National Council of Welfare, *Solving Poverty: Four Cornerstones of a Workable National Strategy for Canada* (Ottawa: National Council of Welfare, 2007). http://www.ncwcnbes.net/en/publications/pub-126.html

---

CHAPTER 1 – DEMOGRAPHICS

1   Statistics Canada, *Projections of the Aboriginal populations, Canada, provinces and territories: 2001 to 2017* (Ottawa: Statistics Canada, 2005), Catalogue no. 91-547-XIE, p. 30. http://www.statcan.ca/english/freepub/91-547-XIE/91-547-XIE2005001.pdf

2   Statistics Canada, *Aboriginal Peoples of Canada: A Demographic Profile,* Analysis Series, 2001 Census (Ottawa: Statistics Canada, 2003), Catalogue no. 96F0030XIE2001007, p. 6. http://www12.statcan.ca/english/census01/products/analytic/companion/abor/pdf/96F0030XIE2001007.pdf

3   Statistics Canada, *A Demographic Profile*, p. 7.

4   Statistics Canada, *A Demographic Profile*, p. 7.

5   Human Resources and Skills Development Canada (HRSDC), *Canadian Youth: Who are they and what do they want*? (Gatineau, Quebec : Human Resources and Skills Development Canada, 2005), Section 10. http://www.youth.gc.ca/yoaux.jsp?&lang=en&flash=1&ta=1&auxpageid=846

6   HRSDC, *Canadian Youth*, Section 10.

7   HRSDC, *Canadian Youth*, Section 10.

8   Statistics Canada, *A Demographic Profile*, p. 8.

9   Median represents the mid-point, with half of the sample less than or equal to the median, and half of the sample greater than or equal to the median.

10 Statistics Canada, *A Demographic Profile*, p. 7.

11 Statistics Canada, *Projections of the Aboriginal populations,* p. 42.

12 Calculated from Statistics Canada, *Projections of the Aboriginal populations,* p. 43.

13 Statistics Canada, *Projections of the Aboriginal populations,* p. 42.

14 Statistics Canada, *Projections of the Aboriginal populations,* p. 43.

15 Systemic racism consists of the policies and practices of organizations which directly or indirectly operate to sustain the advantages of peoples of certain races. This type of racism is more difficult to address because it is implicit and often unconscious. Cultural racism is the basis of both individual and systemic racism, as it is the value system which is embedded in society supporting and allowing discriminatory actions based on perceptions of racial difference, cultural superiority and inferiority. Source: Jennifer Roy, "Acknowledging Racism," ([N.p.: Canadian Race Relations Foundation, [n.d]), p. 1. http://www.crr.ca/divers-files/en/pub/faSh/ePubFaShAckRac.pdf

16 Statistics Canada, *Projections of the Aboriginal populations,* p. 8.

17 Statistics Canada, *Projections of the Aboriginal populations,* pp. 30-31.

18 Statistics Canada, *Projections of the Aboriginal populations,* p. 25.

19   Statistics Canada, *A Demographic Profile*, p. 7.

20   Statistics Canada, *A Demographic Profile*, p. 14.

21   R.S.C. 1985, c. I-5, as am.

22   At the time of writing the B.C. Supreme Court had struck down part of the Indian Act definition of status and ruled that Indian status can be traced entirely through the mother, opening the door to hundreds of thousands of new applications for status. McIvor et al. v. The Registrar, Indian and Northern Affairs Canada et al., 2007 BCSC 26 (CanLII), appeal pending.

23   Michelle M. Mann, *Aboriginal Women: An Issues Backgrounder* (Ottawa: Status of Women Canada, 2005), p. 4. http://www.swc-cfc.gc.ca/resources/consultations/ges09-2005/aboriginal_e.pdf

24   Statistics Canada. Social and Aboriginal Statistics Division.

25   Statistics Canada. Social and Aboriginal Statistics Division.

26   Statistics Canada. Social and Aboriginal Statistics Division.

27   Inuit Tapiriit Kanatami (ITK), Environment and Health Department.

28   Stewart Clatworthy and Mary Jane Norris. "Aboriginal Mobility and Migration: Trends, Recent Patterns, and Implications: 1971-2001," in *Aboriginal Policy Research: Moving Forward Making a Difference (Volume IV), edited by* Jerry P. White, Paul Maxim and Dan Beavon (Toronto: Thompson Educational Publishing, 2007), pp. 210-211.

29   Mary Jane Norris and Stewart Clatworthy, "Aboriginal Mobility and Migration in Canada: Factors, Policy Implications and Responses," Presentation to the Aboriginal Policy Research Conference, Ottawa, March 21-23, 2006. http://sociology.uwo.ca/aprc-crmpa/UPDATED%20MJ%20Norris%20APRC%20Migration%20Mar%2021%202006.swf.

30   Jeremy Hull, *Aboriginal Single Mothers in Canada, 1996: A Statistical Profile* (Ottawa: Indian and Northern Affairs Canada, 2001), pp. x-xi. http://www.ainc-inac.gc.ca/pr/ra/smt/index_e.html

31   ITK, Environment and Health Department.

32   Hull, *Aboriginal Single Mothers*, p. xi.

33   Statistics Canada, *A Demographic Profile*, p. 9.

34   Assembly of First Nations/First Nations Information Governance Committee, *First Nations Regional Longitudinal Health Survey (RHS) 2002/03, Results for Adults, Youth and Children Living in First Nations Communities,* Revised 2nd ed. (Ottawa: First Nations Information Governance Committee, 2007), p. 229. http://rhs-ers.ca/english/pdf/rhs2002-03reports/rhs2002-03-technicalreport-afn.pdf

35   For more on the project see http://www.ecdip.org/fathers/index.htm

36   Jessica Ball and Ron George, "Policies and Practices Affecting Aboriginal Fathers' Involvement with their Children," in *Aboriginal Policy Research: Moving Forward, Making A Difference (Volume III)*, edited by Jerry P. White, Paul Maxim and Dan Beavon (Toronto: Thompson Educational Publishing Inc., 2006), p. 130.

37   Early Childhood Development Intercultural Partnerships, "Indigenous Fatherhood Project: Project Background," (Victoria: Early Childhood Development Intercultural Partnerships, University of Victoria, 2007). http://www.ecdip.org/fathers/index.htm

38   Early Childhood Development Intercultural Partnerships, "Indigenous Fatherhood Project."

39   Statistics Canada, *A Demographic Profile*, p. 9.

40   Pauktuutit Inuit Women of Canada, *The Inuit Way: A Guide to Inuit Culture* (Ottawa: Pauktuutit Inuit Women of Canada, 2006), p. 20. http://www.pauktuutit.ca/pdf/publications/pauktuutit/InuitWay_e.pdf.

41   And dependant on the final outcome of McIvor et al. v. The Registrar, Indian and Northern Affairs Canada et al., 2007 BCSC 26 (CanLII).

CHAPTER 2 – INCOME

1   Median represents the mid-point, with half of the sample less than or equal to the median, and half of the sample greater than or equal to the median.

2   Statistics Canada, *Income Trends in Canada 1980-2005* [CD-ROM] (Ottawa: Statistics Canada, 2007), Catalogue no. 13F0022XIE, Table 2020411.

3   Statistics Canada, Social and Aboriginal Statistics Division.

4   Statistics Canada, Social and Aboriginal Statistics Division.

5   Statistics Canada, Custom tabulation from the Survey of Income and Labour Dynamics, November 2006.

6   Statistics Canada, Custom tabulation from the Survey of Income and Labour Dynamics, November 2006.

7   Statistics Canada, Social and Aboriginal Statistics Division.

8   Statistics Canada, *Family Income Groups(21),Sex(3) and Aboriginal Group of Lone Parent(11) for Lone-parent Census Families in Private Households,for Canada, Provinces and Territories, 2000—20% Sample Data* (table), *Topic-based tabulations: Income of Individuals, Families and Households* (Ottawa: Statistics Canada, June 16, 2004), 2001 Census of Canada, Catalogue No. 97F0020XCB2001065.

9   Assembly of First Nations, *Royal Commission on Aboriginal People at 10 Years: A Report Card* (Ottawa: AFN, 2006), p. 3. http://www.afn.ca/cmslib/general/afn_rcap.pdf

10 Mindy McHardy and Erin O'Sullivan, *First Nations Community Well-Being in Canada: The Community Well-Being Index (CWB) 2001* (Ottawa: Indian and Northern Affairs Canada, 2004), pp. 3-4 and p. 10.

11 Low income cut-offs (LICOs) represent levels of family income where people spend disproportionately large amounts for food, shelter and clothing. LICOs are produced for before-tax and after-tax income. However, only before-tax LICOs are available for the Census. This report uses before-tax LICOs in order to facilitate comparisons to Census data.

12 Statistics Canada, *Selected Income Characteristics (35A), Aboriginal Identity (8), Age Groups (6), Sex (3) and Area of Residence (7) for Population, for Canada, Provinces and Territories, 2001 Census—20% Sample Data* (table), *Topic-based tabulations: Aboriginal Peoples of Canada* (Ottawa: Statistics Canada, December 10, 2003), 2001 Census of Canada, Catalogue No. 97F0011XCB2001046.

13 Statistics Canada, Social and Aboriginal Statistics Division.

14 Statistics Canada, *Selected Income Characteristics (35), Registered Indian Status (3), Age Groups (6) and Sex(3) for Population, for Canada, Provinces, Territories and Census Metropolitan Areas, 2001 Census—20% Sample Data* (table), *Topic-based tabulations: Aboriginal Peoples of Canada* (Ottawa: Statistics Canada, March 24, 2004), 2001 Census of Canada, Catalogue No. 97F0011XCB2001063.

15 Andrew Heisz and Logan McLeod, *Low Income in Census Metropolitan Areas, 1980-2000* (Ottawa: Statistics Canada, 2004), Statistics Canada Catalogue no. 89-613-MIE, p. 89. http://www.statcan.ca/english/research/89-613-MIE/89-613-MIE2004001.htm

16 Heisz and McLeod, *Low Income,* p. 33.

17 Statistics Canada, Custom tabulation from the Survey of Income and Labour Dynamics, November 2006.

18 North-South Partnership for Children, Mamow Sha-way-gi-kay-win, "Immediate Action Needed to Aid First Nation Communities" (Sandy Lake First Nation, ON: North-South Partnership for Children, June 26, 2007). http://www.northsouthpartnership.com/PressReleaseJune26.pdf

19 Assembly of First Nations/First Nations Information Governance Committee, *First Nations Regional Longitudinal Health Survey (RHS) 2002/03, Results for Adults, Youth and Children Living in First Nations Communities,* Revised 2nd ed. (Ottawa: First Nations Information Governance Committee, 2007), p. 230. http://rhs-ers.ca/english/pdf/rhs2002-03reports/rhs2002-03-technicalreport-afn.pdf

20 Pauktuutit Inuit Women of Canada. Issue Paper on Health, Safety and Wellness for the National Aboriginal Women's Summit, June 20-22, 2007. http://www.laa.gov.nl.ca/laa/naws/pdf/Poverty.pdf

21 Ingrid Ledrou and Jean Gervais, "Food Insecurity," *Health Reports.* 16, 3 (May 2005), p. 48, Statistics Canada Catalogue no. 82-003. http://www.statcan.ca/english/freepub/82-003-XIE/0030482-003-XIE.pdf

22 Indian and Northern Affairs Canada (INAC), "Income Assistance Reform—The Way Forward" (Ottawa: INAC, 2006.), p. 26.

23 INAC, "Income Assistance Reform," p. 26.

24 INAC, "Income Assistance Reform," p. 27.

25 INAC, "Income Assistance Reform," p. 4.

26 Federal-Provincial-Territorial (FPT) Directors of Income Support, *Social Assistance Statistical Report: 2005* (Ottawa: Human Resources and Social Development Canada, 2006). http://www.hrsdc.gc.ca/en/cs/sp/sdc/socpol/publications/reports/sd10-3-2004e/page00.shtml

27 INAC, "Income Assistance Reform," p. 22.

28 National Council of Welfare, *Welfare Incomes 2005* (Ottawa: National Council of Welfare, 2006), pp. 44-45.

29 Michelle M. Mann, *Aboriginal Women: An Issues Backgrounder* (Ottawa: Status of Women Canada, 2005), p. 7. http://www.swc-cfc.gc.ca/resources/consultations/ges09-2005/aboriginal_e.pdf

CHAPTER 3 – EMPLOYMENT

1   Statistics Canada, *Selected Labour Force Characteristics (50), Aboriginal Identity (8), Age Groups (5A), Sex (3) and Area of Residence (7) for Population 15 Years and Over, for Canada, Provinces and Territories, 2001 Census—20% Sample Data* (table), *Topic-based tabulations: Aboriginal Peoples of Canada.* (Ottawa: Statistics Canada, November 19, 2003), 2001 Census of Canada, Catalogue No. 97F0011XCB2001044.

2   Statistics Canada, *The Canadian Labour Market at a Glance, 2005* (Ottawa: Statistics Canada, 2006), Catalogue No. 71-222-XIE, p. 95. http://www.statcan.ca/english/freepub/71-222-XIE/71-222-XIE2006001.pdf

3   Statistics Canada, *Selected Labour Force Characteristics* (table).

4   Statistics Canada, *Selected Labour Force Characteristics* (table).

5   INAC, "Income Assistance Reform—The Way Forward" (Ottawa: INAC, 2006.), p. 4.

6   Michael Mendelson, *Aboriginal Peoples and Postsecondary Education in Canada* (Ottawa: Caledon Institute of Social Policy, 2006), p.8. http://www.caledoninst.org/Publications/PDF/595ENG.pdf

7   Statistics Canada. Social and Aboriginal Statistics Division.

8   Statistics Canada, *Selected Income Characteristics (35A), Aboriginal Identity (8), Age Groups (6), Sex (3) and Area of Residence (7) for Population, for Canada, Provinces and Territories, 2001 Census—20% Sample Data* (table), *Topic-based tabulations: Aboriginal Peoples of Canada* (Ottawa: Statistics Canada, December 10, 2003), 2001 Census of Canada, Catalogue No. 97F0011XCB2001046.

9   Coryse Ciceri and Katherine Scott, "The Determinants of Employment among Aboriginal Peoples," in *Aboriginal Policy Research: Moving Forward Making a Difference (Volume III)*, edited by Jerry P. White, Paul Maxim and Dan Beavon (Toronto: Thompson Educational Publishing Inc., 2006), p.17.

10 Jeremy Hull, *Aboriginal Single Mothers in Canada, 1996: A Statistical Profile* (Ottawa: Indian and Northern Affairs Canada, 2001), p. xii. http://www.ainc-inac.gc.ca/pr/ra/smt/index_e.html

11 Statistics Canada, Custom tabulation from the Labour Force Survey, October 2006.

12 Ciceri and Scott, "The Determinants of Employment among Aboriginal Peoples," p. 17.

13 Ciceri and Scott, "The Determinants of Employment among Aboriginal Peoples," p. 17.

14 Ciceri and Scott, "The Determinants of Employment among Aboriginal Peoples," p. 18.

15 Ciceri and Scott, "The Determinants of Employment among Aboriginal Peoples," p. 19.

16 Calculated from Statistics Canada, *Selected Income Characteristics, Aboriginal Identity* (table).

17 Statistics Canada, *Selected Labour Force Characteristics* (table).

18 Data in this section is from Statistics Canada, Custom tabulation from the Labour Force Survey, October 2006, unless otherwise noted.

19 Ciceri and Scott, "The Determinants of Employment among Aboriginal Peoples," p. 8.

20 Ciceri and Scott, "The Determinants of Employment among Aboriginal Peoples," p. 23.

CHAPTER 4 – EDUCATION, LANGUAGE AND CULTURE

1   OECD, *Starting Strong II: Early Childhood Education and Care* (Paris: OECD Publications, 2006), p. 104.

2   Indian and Northern Affairs Canada (INAC), "Income Assistance Reform—The Way Forward" (Ottawa: INAC, 2006), p. 4.

3   Congress of Aboriginal Peoples, "Child Care Spaces Initiative," *ELCC Bulletin* No. 4 (Fall 2006).

4   Jennifer Dickson, Pauktuutit Inuit Women of Canada, personal correspondence, August 1, 2007.

5   Canada, *Early childhood development activities and expenditures: Early learning and child care activities and expenditures, 2003-2004* (Ottawa: Government of Canada, 2005), pp. 68-70. http://www.socialunion.ca/SP544114E.pdf

6   Canada, *Early childhood development activities and expenditures,* pp. 65-66.

7   Health Canada, "Early Childhood Development Strategy for Aboriginal Children: Expansion of Aboriginal Head Start (AHS)" (Ottawa: Health Canada, 2005), accessed June 25, 2007. http://www.hc-sc.gc.ca/fnih-spni/famil/develop/ahs-papa_expansion_e.html

8   Native Council of Canada, *Native Child Care: the Circle of Care* (Ottawa: Native Council of Canada, 1990).

9 INAC, *Canada-Aboriginal Peoples Roundtable: Lifelong Learning Background Paper* (Ottawa: Government of Canada, 2004), p. 2. http://aboriginalroundtable.ca/sect/lrng/bckpr/INAC_BgPaper_LLL1_2_e.pdf

10 Michael Mendelson, *Aboriginal Peoples and Postsecondary Education in Canada* (Ottawa: Caledon Institute of Social Policy, 2006), p. 18. http://www.caledoninst.org/Publications/PDF/595ENG.pdf

11 Assembly of First Nations (AFN), *Background Paper on Lifelong Learning* (Ottawa: AFN, 2004), p. 2. http://www.afn.ca/cmslib/general/LLL-BP.pdf

12 Jeremy Hull, *Post-Secondary Education and Labour Market Outcomes: Canada, 2001* (Ottawa: Indian and Northern Affairs Canada, 2005), pp. 51-52. http://www.ainc-inac.gc.ca/pr/ra/pse/01/01_e.pdf

13 Statistics Canada, Social and Aboriginal Statistics Division.

14 National Aboriginal Health Organization (NAHO), "First Nations Center Survey of Youth Health Issues and Priorities," accessed August 8, 2007. http://www.naho.ca/firstnations/english/nations_circle_reports_stats.php

15 Laura Metcalfe, *Exploring Empowering Education for Marginalized Youth in Toronto* (Toronto: For Youth Initiative, 2003), p. 20. http://www.foryouth.ca/resources/downloads/empowering_report.pdf

16 Metcalfe, *Education for Marginalized Youth, p.* 20.

17 Paul Maxim and Jerry White, "School Completion and Workforce Transitions," in *Aboriginal Policy Research: Moving Forward Making a Difference (Volume 3)*, edited by Jerry P. White, Paul Maxim and Dan Beavon (Toronto: Thompson Educational Publishing Inc., 2006), pp. 38-39.

18 INAC, *Roundtable: Lifelong Learning*, p. 16.

19 Mendelson, *Aboriginal Peoples and Postsecondary Education,* p. 21.

20 INAC, *Roundtable: Lifelong Learning*, p. 2.

21 INAC, *Roundtable: Lifelong Learning*, p. 16.

22 INAC, *Roundtable: Lifelong Learning*, p. 16.

23 Statistics Canada, *Education in Canada: Raising the standard*, Analysis Series, 2001 Census (Ottawa: Statistics Canada, 2003), Catalogue no. 96F0030XIE2001012, p. 16. http://www12.statcan.ca/english/census01/Products/Analytic/companion/educ/pdf/96F0030XIE2001012.pdf

24 Jeremy Hull, *Aboriginal Women: A Profile from the 2001 Census* (Ottawa: Indian and Northern Affairs Canada, 2006), p. 44. http://www.ainc-inac.gc.ca/pr/pub/abw/abw_e.pdf

25 Hull, *Aboriginal Women: A Profile*, pp. 44-45.

26 AFN, National Chief Phil Fontaine, Opening remarks (Gatineau, Quebec: AFN Policy Forum/Special Chiefs Assembly, May 22, 2007).

27 Maxim and White, "School Completion and Workforce Transitions", p. 35.

28 Metcalfe, *Education for Marginalized Youth*, p. 20.

29 Statistics Canada, "Aboriginal Peoples Survey: Well-being of the non-reserve Aboriginal population," *The Daily* (Ottawa: Statistics Canada, September 24, 2003), Catalogue no. 11-001-XIE. http://www.statcan.ca/Daily/English/030924/d030924.pdf

30 Canada Millennium Scholarship Foundation, *Changing Course: Improving Aboriginal Access to Post-Secondary Education in Canada* (Montreal: Canada Millennium Scholarship Foundation, 2005), p. 4. http://www.millenniumscholarships.ca/images/Publications/mrn-changing-course-en.pdf

31 AFN, *Lifelong Learning*, p. 15.

32 Mary Jane Norris, "Aboriginal Languages in Canada: Trends and Perspectives on Maintenance and Revitalization," in *Aboriginal Policy Research: Moving Forward Making a Difference (Volume 3)*, edited by Jerry P. White, Paul Maxim and Dan Beavon (Toronto: Thompson Educational Publishing, 2006), p. 198.

33 Norris, "Aboriginal Languages," pp. 199-200.

34 Norris, "Aboriginal Languages", p. 207.

35 Stephen Wurm, ed., *Atlas of the World's Languages in Danger of Disappearing,* (Paris: UNESCO, 1996), p. 23.

36 Inuit Tapiriit Kanatami (ITK), *Backgrounder on Inuit and Education* (Ottawa: ITK, 2004), p. 12. http://www.aboriginalroundtable.ca/sect/lrng/bckpr/ITK_BgPaper_LLL1_2_e.pdf

37 Human Resources and Skills Development Canada, *Canadian Youth: Who are they and what do they want?* (Gatineau, Quebec : Human Resources and Skills Development Canada, 2005), Section 10. http://www.youth.gc.ca/yoaux.jsp?&lang=en&flash=1&ta=1&auxpageid=846

38 ITK, *Inuit and Education*, p. 12.

39   Canada, Royal Commission on Aboriginal Peoples, *Highlights from the Report of the Royal Commission on Aboriginal Peoples* (Ottawa: Minister of Supply and Services, 1996). http://www.ainc-inac.gc.ca/ch/rcap/rpt/gs_e.html

40   AFN, "Fiscal Fairness for First Nations." (Ottawa: AFN, [n.d]). www.afn.ca/misc/fffn.pdf

41   Michael Mendelson, *Improving Primary and Secondary Education on Reserves in Canada* (Ottawa: Caledon Institute of Social Policy, 2006), p. 2. http://www.caledoninst.org/Publications/PDF/608ENG.pdf

42   *The Canada Gazette,* Part III, Vol. 29, No. 2 (31 January 2007).

CHAPTER 5 – HEALTH, WELLNESS AND SAFETY

1   Health Canada, *Health Sectoral Session: Background Paper* (Ottawa: Government of Canada, 2004), p. 5. http://www.aboriginalroundtable.ca/sect/hlth/bckpr/HC_BgPaper_e.pdf

2   Health Canada, *Health Sectoral Session: Background Paper*, p. 6.

3   Assembly of First Nations (AFN)/First Nations Information Governance Committee, *First Nations Regional Longitudinal Health Survey (RHS) 2002/03, Results for Adults, Youth and Children Living in First Nations Communities,* Revised 2nd ed. (Ottawa: First Nations Information Governance Committee, 2007), p. 261. http://rhs-ers.ca/english/pdf/rhs2002-03reports/rhs2002-03-technicalreport-afn.pdf

4   Health Canada, "Diabetes: Aboriginal Diabetes Initiative" (Ottawa: Health Canada, 2007). http://www.hc-sc.gc.ca/fnih-spni/diseases-maladies/diabete/index_e.html

5   Environics Research Group, *2004 Baseline Study Among First Nations On-reserve and Inuit in the North,* quoted in Health Canada, "Tobacco: Facts on Smoking Rates" (Ottawa: Health Canada, 2005). http://www.hc-sc.gc.ca/fnih-spni/substan/tobac-tabac/index_e.html#facts

6   Health Canada, *A Second Diagnostic on the Health of First Nations and Inuit People in Canada* (Ottawa: Health Canada, 1999).

7   Janet, C. Curry, *Best Practices: Treatment and Rehabilitation for Youth with Substance Use Problems* (Ottawa: Health Canada, 2001), p. 16, quoting Canadian Centre on Substance Abuse and Centre for Addiction and Mental Health, *Canadian Profile: Alcohol, Tobacco and Other Drugs*, Vols. 1997 and 1999. http://www.hc-sc.gc.ca/hl-vs/alt_formats/hecs-sesc/pdf/pubs/adp-apd/youth-jeunes/youth-jeunes_e.pdf

8   Curry, *Best Practices*, p. 16.

9   Alberta, Premier's Task Force on Crystal Meth, *Fighting Back* (Edmonton: Government of Alberta, 2006). http://www.premier.alberta.ca/cmeth

10   Madeleine Dion Stout and Gregory D. Kipling, *Emerging Priorities for the Health of First Nations and Inuit Children and Youth* (Ottawa: First Nations and Inuit Health Branch (FNIHB), Health Canada, 1999). http://www.hc-sc.gc.ca/fnih-spni/pubs/develop/1999_priorit-child-enfant/index_e.html

11   Health Canada, "Statistical Profile on the Health of First Nations in Canada: Highlights of First Nations Health Statistics" (Ottawa: Health Canada, 2005). http://www.hc-sc.gc.ca/fnih-spni/pubs/gen/stats_profil_e.html

12   AFN/First Nations Information Governance Committee, *RHS*, p. 265.

13   Health Canada, "HIV and AIDS: Facts on HIV and AIDS in First Nations and Inuit Populations" (Ottawa: Health Canada, 2006). http://www.hc-sc.gc.ca/fnih-spni/diseases-maladies/aids-sida/index_e.html

14   Curry, *Best Practices*, p. 16.

15   Health Canada, "Suicide Prevention: Facts on Suicide Rates" (Ottawa: Health Canada, 2003). http://www.hc-sc.gc.ca/fnih-spni/promotion/suicide/index_e.html

16   AFN/First Nations Information Governance Committee, *RHS*, p. 217.

17   Dion Stout and Kipling, *Emerging Priorities*.

18   AFN/First Nations Information Governance Committee, *RHS*, p. 221.

19   Inuit Tapiriit Kanatami (ITK), Backgrounder on Inuit Health (Ottawa: ITK, 2004), p. 2. http://www.aboriginalroundtable.ca/sect/hlth/bckpr/ITK_BgPaper_e.pdf

20   Health Canada, *Health Sectoral Session: Background Paper*, p. 6.

21   AFN/First Nations Information Governance Committee, *RHS*, p. 247.

22   AFN/First Nations Information Governance Committee, *RHS*, p. 239.

23 Martin Turcotte and Grant Schellenberg, *A Portrait of Seniors in Canada* (Ottawa: Statistics Canada, 2007), Statistics Canada Catalogue no. 89-519-XPE, p. 223. http://www.statcan.ca/english/freepub/89-519-XIE/89-519-XIE2006001.pdf

24 Health Canada, *A Statistical Profile on the Health of First Nations in Canada* (Ottawa: Health Canada, 2002), p. 43.

25 Michelle M. Mann, *Aboriginal Women: An Issues Backgrounder* (Ottawa: Status of Women Canada, 2005), p. 6. http://www.swc-cfc.gc.ca/resources/consultations/ges09-2005/aboriginal_e.pdf

26 Statistics Canada, *Measuring Violence Against Women: Statistical Trends 2006* (Ottawa: Statistics Canada, 2006), Catalogue no. 85-570-XIE, p. 65 and 67. http://www.statcan.ca/english/research/85-570-XIE/85-570-XIE2006001.pdf

27 Jodi-Anne Brzozowski, Andrea Taylor-Butts and Sara Johnson, "Victimization and offending among the Aboriginal population in Canada," *Juristat*. 26, 3 (June 2006), Statistics Canada Catalogue no. 85-002-XIE, p. 7. http://www.statcan.ca/english/freepub/85-002-XIE/85-002-XIE2006003.pdf

28 Mann, *Aboriginal Women,* p. 2.

29 Mann, *Aboriginal Women,* p. 3.

30 Amnesty International Canada, *Canada: Stolen Sisters - A Human Rights Response to Discrimination and Violence against Indigenous Women in Canada* (Ottawa: Amnesty International, 2004), p. 2. http://www.amnesty.ca/campaigns/resources/amr2000304.pdf

31 Amnesty International Canada, *Stolen Sisters*, pp. 23-24.

32 Mann, *Aboriginal Women,* p. 3.

33 AFN/First Nations Information Governance Committee, *RHS*, Chapters 16-25.

34 Statistics Canada, *A Profile of Canada's Métis Population* (Ottawa: Statistics Canada, 2004), Slide 20. http://www.aboriginalroundtable.ca/sect/stscan/Metis_e.pdf

35 Canada Mortgage and Housing Corporation, *Aboriginal Housing Background Paper – Part ii* (Ottawa: Indian and Northern Affairs Canada, 2004), p. 31. http://www.aboriginalroundtable.ca/sect/hsng/bckpr/INAC_annexb_e.pdf

36 Canadian Institute for Health Information, *Improving the Health of Canadians* (Ottawa: Canadian Institute for Health Information, 2004), p. 78. http://secure.cihi.ca/cihiweb/dispPage.jsp?cw_page=PG_39_E&cw_topic=39&cw_rel=AR_322_E

37 AFN, *Background Paper on First Nations Health* ([Ottawa]: AFN, 2004), p. 1. http://www.aboriginalroundtable.ca/sect/hlth/bckpr/AFN_BgPaper_e.pdf

38 ITK, *Inuit Health*, p. 8.

39 For example, see a description of some successful initiatives in First Nations integrated primary and continuing health care in AFN, *First Nations Health*, p. 5.

40 AFN, *First Nations Health*, p. 5.

41 ITK, *Inuit Health*, p. 8.

42 Canadian Centre on Substance Abuse, *Youth Overview,* (Ottawa: Canadian Centre on Substance Abuse, 2007). http://www.ccsa.ca/CCSA/EN/Topics/Populations/YouthOverview.htm

43 ITK, *Inuit Health*, p. 6.

44 Alastair MacPhee, personal correspondence, August 3, 2007.

45 Alberta, *Fighting Back.*

46 Dr. Valerie Gideon, personal correspondence, January 1, 2007.

47 ITK, *Inuit Health*, p. 7.

48 *The Constitution Act, 1982,* being Schedule B to the *Canada Act 1982* (U.K.), 1982, c. 11.

49 *Indian Act*, R.S.C. 1985, c.I-5, as amended s.81(1)(a).

CHAPTER 6 - HOUSING

1 Stewart Clatworthy and Mary Jane Norris, "Aboriginal Mobility and Migration: Trends, Recent Patterns, and Implications: 1971-2001" in *Aboriginal Policy Research: Moving Forward Making a Difference (Volume IV), edited by* Jerry P. White, Paul Maxim and Dan Beavon (Toronto: Thompson Educational Publishing, 2007), p. 228.

2   Indigenous Network on Economics and Trade (INET), et al, *Independent Indigenous Submission to the United Nations Committee on Economic, Social and Cultural Rights in Response to Canada's Periodic Reports,* Joint Submission to the United Nations Committee on Economic, Social and Cultural Rights, 36th Session, May 2006, p. 36. http://www.ohchr.org/english/bodies/cescr/docs/info-ngos/independentindigenous.pdf

3   Canada Mortgage and Housing Corporation (CMHC), *Aboriginal Housing Background Paper – Part ii* (Ottawa: Indian and Northern Affairs Canada, 2004), p. 19. http://www.aboriginalroundtable.ca/sect/hsng/bckpr/INAC_annexb_e.pdf

4   City of Toronto, City Planning Division, *Perspectives on Housing Affordability* (Toronto: City of Toronto, 2006), p. 21. http://www.toronto.ca/planning/pdf/housing_afford.pdf

5   CMHC, *2001 Census Housing Series: Issue 6 Revised, Aboriginal Households,* Socio-economic Series, No. 04-036 (Ottawa: CMHC, 2004), p. 3. http://www.cmhc-schl.gc.ca/odpub/pdf/63695.pdf

6   CMHC, *Aboriginal Households,* p. 3.

7   A census metropolitan area (CMA) or a census agglomeration (CA) is formed by one or more adjacent municipalities centred on a large urban area (known as the urban core). The census population count of the urban core is at least 10,000 to form a census agglomeration and at least 100,000 to form a census metropolitan area.

8   CMHC, *Aboriginal Households,* p. 3.

9   Inuit Tapiriit Kanatami (ITK), Environment and Health Department.

10 ITK, *Backgrounder on Inuit and Housing* (Ottawa: ITK, 2004), p. 5. http://www.aboriginalroundtable.ca/sect/hsng/bckpr/ITK_BgPaper_e.pdf

11 Shelley Trevethan, et al, *The Needs of Inuit Offenders in Federal Correctional Facilities* (Ottawa: Correctional Service of Canada, 2004). http://www.csc-scc.gc.ca/text/rsrch/reports/r142/r142_e.shtml

12 CMHC, *Aboriginal Housing Background Paper* (Ottawa: Indian and Northern Affairs Canada, 2004), p. 3. http://www.aboriginalroundtable.ca/sect/hsng/bckpr/INAC_BgPaper_e.pdf

13 Canada, Royal Commission on Aboriginal Peoples, *Urban Survivors, Aboriginal Street Youth: Vancouver, Winnipeg & Montreal (Kaptitipis e-pimohteyahk: Vancouver, Winnipeg and Montreal)*, by Lauri Gilchrist and R. Anthony Winchester, RCAP Research Reports, Urban, in *For Seven Generations: An Information Legacy of the Royal Commission on Aboriginal Peoples* [CD-ROM] (Ottawa: Libraxus, 1997).

14 CMHC, *Environmental Scan On Youth Homelessness*, Socio-economic Series, Issue 86 (Ottawa: CMHC, 2001), p. 1. http://www.cmhc.ca/publications/en/rh-pr/socio/socio086.pdf

15 CMHC, *Youth Homelessness*, p. 1.

16 CMHC, *Aboriginal Housing Background Paper*, p. 2.

17 Indian Affairs and Northern Affairs Canada (INAC), "Fact Sheet: Aboriginal Housing" (Ottawa: INAC, 2006), accessed June 29, 2007. http://www.ainc-inac.gc.ca/pr/info/fnsocec/abhsg_e.html

18 CMHC, *Aboriginal Housing Background Paper*, p. 4.

19 INAC, *Basic Departmental Data 2003* (Ottawa: INAC, 2004), p. 61. http://www.ainc-inac.gc.ca/pr/sts/bdd03/bdd03_e.pdf

20 CBC News, "Aboriginal peoples, 10 years after the royal commission," November 21, 2006. http://www.cbc.ca/news/background/aboriginals/status-report2006.html

21 Health Canada, "Drinking water advisories." (Ottawa: Health Canada, 2007), accessed June 18, 2007. http://www.hc-sc.gc.ca/fnih-spni/promotion/water-eau/advis-avis_concern_e.html

22 30 & 31 Victoria, c. 3 (U.K.).

23 R.S.C. 1985, c. I-5.

24 Michelle M. Mann, *Aboriginal Women: An Issues Backgrounder* (Ottawa: Status of Women Canada, 2005), p. 5. http://www.swc-cfc.gc.ca/resources/consultations/ges09-2005/aboriginal_e.pdf

25 Mann, *Aboriginal Women*, pp. 4-5.

26 R.S. 1985, c. H-6.

27 Mann, *Aboriginal Women*, p. 5.

CHAPTER 7 – CHILDREN AND YOUTH "IN CARE"

1   C. Blackstock and N. Trocmé, *Community Based Child Welfare for Aboriginal Children: Supporting Resilience through Structural Change* (Toronto: CECW, 2004), p. 4. www.cecw-cepb.ca/files/file/en/communityBasedCWAboriginalChildren.pdf

2   P. Gough, et al, *Pathways to the Overrepresentation of Aboriginal Children in Care,* CECW Information Sheet #23E (Toronto: University of Toronto, 2005), p. 1. www.cecw-cepb.ca/files/file/en/AboriginalChildren23E.pdf

3   See, for example, "Chapter 13—The Impacts of Residential Schools" in Assembly of First Nations/First Nations Information Governance Committee, *First Nations Regional Longitudinal Health Survey (RHS) 2002/03, Results for Adults, Youth and Children Living in First Nations Communities,* Revised 2nd ed. (Ottawa: First Nations Information Governance Committee, 2007). http://rhs-ers.ca/english/pdf/rhs2002-03reports/rhs2002-03-technicalreport-afn.pdf.

4   R.S.C. 1985, c. I-5.

5   K. Richard, "A commentary against Aboriginal to non-Aboriginal adoption," *First Peoples Child and Family Review* 1, 1 (September 2004), p. 102. http://www.fncfcs.com/pubs/vol1num1/Richard_pp101-109.pdf

6   Blackstock and Trocmé, *Community Based Child Welfare,* p. 6.

7   Gough, et al., *Pathways,* p. 1.

8   First Nations Child and Family Caring Society of Canada, *Non Discrimination and Diversity,* submission to the United Nations Committee on the Rights of the Child, August 29, 2003, p. 3. http://www.fncfcs.com/docs/UnitedNationsMay2004.pdf

9   Richard, "Aboriginal to non-Aboriginal adoption," pp. 102-103.

10 Richard, "Aboriginal to non-Aboriginal adoption," p. 101.

11 Statistics Canada, *Population Reporting an Aboriginal Identity, by Age Group, by Province and Territory (2001 Census)* (table). *Summary Tables,* accessed July 4, 2007. http://www.statcan.ca/l01/cst01/demo40a.htm?sdi=aboriginal%20identity

12 British Columbia, Ministry of Child and Family Development, *Annual Service Plan Report 2005/06* (Victoria: Government of British Columbia, 2006), p. 4. http://www.bcbudget.gov.bc.ca/Annual_Reports/2005_2006/cfd/cfd.pdf

13 Bruce Hallet, *Aboriginal Peoples in Manitoba* (Winnipeg: Service Canada, 2006), p. 42. http://www1.servicecanada.gc.ca/en/mb/aboriginal-profile/aboriginals.pdf

14 Blackstock and Trocmé, *Community Based Child Welfare,* p. 5.

15 Assembly of First Nations (AFN), "Canadian Human Rights complaint on First Nations child welfare filed today by Assembly of First Nations and First Nations Child and Family Caring Society of Canada" (Ottawa: AFN, February 23, 2007). http://www.afn.ca/article.asp?id=3374

16 AFN, "Assembly of First Nations signs child welfare partnership agreement and launches Leadership Action Plan on First Nations Child Welfare" (Ottawa: AFN, November 21, 2006). http://www.afn.ca/article.asp?id=3139

17 Nancy MacDonald and Judy MacDonald, "Reflections of a Mi'kmaq social worker on a quarter of a century work in First Nations child welfare," *First Peoples Child and Family Review* 3, 1 (2007), p. 42. http://www.fncfcs.com/pubs/vol3num1/MacDonald_MacDonald_pp34.pdf

18 Phil Fontaine, "The Native Fiscal Imbalance," *The Globe and Mail,* October 30, 2006, p. A19.

19 P. Gough, C. Blackstock, and N. Bala, *Jurisdiction and funding models for Aboriginal child and family service agencies,* CECW Information Sheet #30E (Toronto: University of Toronto, 2005), p. 1. http://www.cecw-cepb.ca/files/file/en/JurisdictionandFunding30E.pdf

CHAPTER 8 - JUSTICE

1   Office of the Correctional Investigator (OCI), *Annual Report of the Office of the Correctional Investigator 2005-2006* (Ottawa: Minister of Public Works and Government Services Canada, 2006), p. 11. http://www.ocf-bec.gc.ca/reports/AR200506_download_e.asp

2   OCI, "Backgrounder: Aboriginal Inmates" (Ottawa: OCI, 2006), accessed July 10, 2007. http://www.oci-bec.gc.ca/newsroom/bk-AR0506_e.asp

3   OCI, "Aboriginal Inmates."

4   OCI, *Annual Report,* p. 11.

5   OCI, "Report Finds Evidence of Systemic Discrimination Against Aboriginal Inmates in Canada's Prisons" (Ottawa: OCI, October 16, 2006). www.oci-bec.gc.ca/newsroom/releases/20061016_e.asp

6   Larry Chartrand and Celeste McKay, *A Review of Research on Criminal Victimization and First Nations, Métis and Inuit Peoples 1990 to 2001* (Ottawa: Department of Justice Canada, 2006), p. 43. http://www.justice.gc.ca/en/ps/rs/rep/2006/rr06-vic1/rr06-vic1.pdf

7   National Council of Welfare, *Justice and the Poor* (Ottawa: National Council of Welfare, 2000). http://www.ncwcnbes.net/en/publications/pub-111.html

8   Jodi-Anne Brzozowski, Andrea Taylor-Butts and Sara Johnson, "Victimization and offending among the Aboriginal population in Canada," *Juristat*. 26, 3 (June 2006), Statistics Canada Catalogue no. 85-002-XIE, p. 14. http://www.statcan.ca/english/freepub/85-002-XIE/85-002-XIE2006003.pdf

9   OCI, "Aboriginal Inmates."

10   Jeff Latimer and Laura Casey Foss, *A One-Day Snapshot of Aboriginal Youth in Custody Across Canada: Phase II* (Ottawa: Department of Justice Canada, 2004), p. iii. http://justice-canada.net/en/ps/rs/rep/2004/snap2/snapshot2.pdf

11   Three per cent were unknown. Latimer and Casey Foss, *One-Day Snapshot,* p. 11.

12   Latimer and Casey Foss, *One-Day Snapshot,* p. 20.

13   Brzozowski, Taylor-Butts and Johnson, "Victimization and Offending," p. 1.

14   Chartrand and McKay, *Criminal Victimization*, Chapter 6.

15   Nicole Eshkakogan, "Young Aboriginal Women Missing: Who Cares?" AYN News, April 1, 2003. http://www.ayn.ca/ViewNews.aspx?id=267

16   For more information, see the NWAC website. http://www.nwac-hq.org/en/background.html

17   Canada, Royal Commission on Aboriginal Peoples, Report of the Royal Commission on Aboriginal Peoples, Vol. 3: Gathering Strength (Ottawa: Minister of Supply and Services, 1996), pp. 62-63. http://www.ainc-inac.gc.ca/ch/rcap/

18   Canadian Criminal Justice Association, *Aboriginal Peoples and the Criminal Justice System* (Ottawa: Canadian Criminal Justice Association, 2000). http://www.ccja-acjp.ca/en/aborit.html

19   Latimer and Casey Foss, *One-Day Snapshot,* p. 11.

20   R.S.C. 1985, c. C-46.

21   S.C. 2002, c. 1.

22   Data for youth cleared by alternate measures is likely undercounted, as not all police services keep records on youth dealt with in this manner.

23   Brzozowski, Taylor-Butts and Johnson, "Victimization and Offending," p. 11.

24   Brzozowski, Taylor-Butts and Johnson, "Victimization and Offending," p. 27.

Alberta, Premier's Task Force on Crystal Meth. *Fighting Back.* Edmonton: Government of Alberta, 2006. http://www.premier.alberta.ca/cmeth

The Alliance to End Homelessness. *Experiencing Homelessness: The First Report Card on Homelessness in Ottawa, 2004.* Ottawa: The Alliance to End Homelessness, 2005. http://www.endhomelessnessottawa.ca/pdf/Report_Card_on_Homelessness_in_Ottawa_2004.pdf

Amnesty International Canada. *Canada: Stolen Sisters - A Human Rights Response to Discrimination and Violence against Indigenous Women in Canada.* Ottawa: Amnesty International, 2004. http://www.amnesty.ca/campaigns/resources/amr2000304.pdf

Assembly of First Nations (AFN). *Background Paper on First Nations Health.* [Ottawa]: AFN, 2004. http://www.aboriginalroundtable.ca/sect/hlth/bckpr/AFN_BgPaper_e.pdf

AFN. *Background Paper on Lifelong Learning.* Ottawa: AFN, 2004. http://www.afn.ca/cmslib/general/LLL-BP.pdf

AFN. "Assembly of First Nations signs child welfare partnership agreement and launches Leadership Action Plan on First Nations Child Welfare." Ottawa: AFN, November 21, 2006. http://www.afn.ca/article.asp?id=3139

AFN. *Royal Commission on Aboriginal People at 10 Years: A Report Card.* Ottawa: AFN, 2006. http://www.afn.ca/cmslib/general/afn_rcap.pdf

AFN. "Canadian Human Rights complaint on First Nations child welfare filed today by Assembly of First Nations and First Nations Child and Family Caring Society of Canada." Ottawa: AFN, February 23, 2007. http://www.afn.ca/article.asp?id=3374

AFN, National Chief Phil Fontaine. Opening remarks. Gatineau, Quebec: AFN Policy Forum/Special Chiefs Assembly, May 22, 2007. http://www.afn.ca/article.asp?id=3639

AFN. "First Nations Call On All Canadians To Stand With Us On June 29th, 2007." Gatineau, Quebec: AFN, May 23, 2007. http://www.afn.ca/article.asp?id=3635

AFN. "Fiscal Fairness for First Nations." Ottawa: AFN, [n.d.]. www.afn.ca/misc/fffn.pdf

Assembly of First Nations/First Nations Information Governance Committee. *First Nations Regional Longitudinal Health Survey (RHS) 2002/03, Results for Adults, Youth and Children Living in First Nations Communities.* Revised 2nd ed. Ottawa: First Nations Information Governance Committee, 2007. http://rhs-ers.ca/english/pdf/rhs2002-03reports/rhs2002-03-technicalreport-afn.pdf.

Ball, Jessica and Ron George. "Policies and Practices Affecting Aboriginal Fathers' Involvement with their Children." In *Aboriginal Policy Research: Moving Forward, Making A Difference (Volume III)*, edited by Jerry P. White, Paul Maxim and Dan Beavon. Toronto: Thompson Educational Publishing Inc., 2006.

Blackstock, C. and N. Trocmé. *Community Based Child Welfare for Aboriginal Children: Supporting Resilience through Structural Change.* Toronto: CECW, 2004. www.cecw-cepb.ca/files/file/en/communityBasedCWAboriginalChildren.pdf

British Columbia, Ministry of Child and Family Development. *Annual Service Plan Report 2005/06.* Victoria: Government of British Columbia, 2006. http://www.bcbudget.gov.bc.ca/Annual_Reports/2005_2006/cfd/cfd.pdf

Brzozowski, Jodi-Anne, Andrea Taylor-Butts and Sara Johnson. "Victimization and offending among the Aboriginal population in Canada." *Juristat.* 26, 3 (June 2006). Statistics Canada Catalogue no. 85-002-XIE. http://www.statcan.ca/english/freepub/85-002-XIE/85-002-XIE2006003.pdf

Calverley, Donna. "Youth custody and community services in Canada, 2003/04." *Juristat*, 26, 2 (March 2006). Statistics Canada Catalogue no. 85-002-XPE. http://www.statcan.ca/english/freepub/85-002-XIE/0020685-002-XIE.pdf

Canada. Royal Commission on Aboriginal Peoples. *Report of the Royal Commission on Aboriginal Peoples.* 5 vols. Ottawa: Minister of Supply and Services, 1996. http://www.ainc-inac.gc.ca/ch/rcap/

Canada. Royal Commission on Aboriginal Peoples. *Highlights from the Report of the Royal Commission on Aboriginal Peoples.* Ottawa: Minister of Supply and Services, 1996. http://www.ainc-inac.gc.ca/ch/rcap/rpt/index_e.html

Canada. Royal Commission on Aboriginal Peoples. *Urban Survivors, Aboriginal Street Youth: Vancouver, Winnipeg & Montreal (Kaptitipis e-pimohteyahk: Vancouver,Winnipeg and Montreal)*, by Lauri Gilchrist and R. Anthony Winchester. RCAP Research Reports. Urban. In *For Seven Generations: An Information Legacy of the Royal Commission on Aboriginal Peoples* [CD-ROM]. Ottawa: Libraxus, 1997.

Canada. *Early childhood development activities and expenditures: Early learning and child care activities and expenditures, 2003-2004.* Ottawa: Government of Canada, 2005. http://www.socialunion.ca/SP544114E.pdf

Canada Millennium Scholarship Foundation. *Changing Course: Improving Aboriginal Access to Post-Secondary Education in Canada.* Montreal: Canada Millennium Scholarship Foundation, 2005. http://www.millenniumscholarships.ca/images/Publications/mrn-changing-course-en.pdf

Canada Mortgage and Housing Corporation (CMHC). *Environmental Scan On Youth Homelessness*. Socio-economic Series, Issue 86. Ottawa: CMHC, 2001. http://www.cmhc.ca/publications/en/rh-pr/socio/socio086.pdf

CMHC. *Aboriginal Housing Background Paper*. Ottawa: Indian and Northern Affairs Canada, 2004. http://www.aboriginalroundtable.ca/sect/hsng/bckpr/INAC_BgPaper_e.pdf

CMHC. *Aboriginal Housing Background Paper – Part ii*. Ottawa: Indian and Northern Affairs Canada, 2004. http://www.aboriginalroundtable.ca/sect/hsng/bckpr/INAC_annexb_e.pdf

CMHC. *2001 Census Housing Series: Issue 6 Revised, Aboriginal Households*. Socio-economic Series, No. 04-036. Ottawa: CMHC, 2004. http://www.cmhc-schl.gc.ca/odpub/pdf/63695.pdf

Canadian Centre on Substance Abuse. *Youth Overview*. Ottawa: Canadian Centre on Substance Abuse, 2007. http://www.ccsa.ca/CCSA/EN/Topics/Populations/YouthOverview.htm

Canadian Criminal Justice Association. *Aboriginal Peoples and the Criminal Justice System*. Ottawa: Canadian Criminal Justice Association, 2000. http://www.ccja-acjp.ca/en/aborit.html

Canadian Human Rights Act, R.S.C. 1985, c. H-6.

Canadian Institute for Health Information. *Improving the Health of Canadians*. Ottawa: Canadian Institute for Health Information, 2004. http://secure.cihi.ca/cihiweb/dispPage.jsp?cw_page=PG_39_E&cw_topic=39&cw_rel=AR_322_E

CBC News. "Aboriginal peoples, 10 years after the royal commission". November 21, 2006. http://www.cbc.ca/news/background/aboriginals/status-report2006.html

CBC News. "CYFN withdraws from Children's Act review". March 24, 2006. http://www.cbc.ca/canada/north/story/2006/03/24/childact-cyfn24032006.html

Chartrand, Larry and Celeste McKay. *A Review of Research on Criminal Victimization and First Nations, Métis and Inuit Peoples 1990 to 2001*. Ottawa: Department of Justice Canada, 2006. http://www.justice.gc.ca/en/ps/rs/rep/2006/rr06-vic1/rr06-vic1.pdf

Ciceri, Coryse and Katherine Scott. "The Determinants of Employment among Aboriginal Peoples." In *Aboriginal Policy Research: Moving Forward Making a Difference (Volume 3)*, edited by Jerry P. White, Paul Maxim and Dan Beavon. Toronto: Thompson Educational Publishing Inc., 2006.

City of Calgary, Community & Neighbourhood Services. *Results of the 2006 Count of Homeless Persons in Calgary*. Calgary: City of Calgary, 2006. http://intraspec.ca/2006_calgary_homeless_count.pdf

City of Toronto, City Planning Division. *Perspectives on Housing Affordability*. Toronto: City of Toronto, 2006. http://www.toronto.ca/planning/pdf/housing_afford.pdf

Clatworthy, Stewart and Mary Jane Norris. "Aboriginal Mobility and Migration: Trends, Recent Patterns, and Implications: 1971-2001." In *Aboriginal Policy Research: Moving Forward Making a Difference (Volume IV), edited by* Jerry P. White, Paul Maxim and Dan Beavon (Toronto: Thompson Educational Publishing, 2007).

Congress of Aboriginal Peoples. *Background Paper for the Accountability for Results Round Table, January 25&26, 2005: A Proposed Solution*. Ottawa: Congress of Aboriginal Peoples, 2005. http://www.aboriginalroundtable.com/sect/acnt/bckpr/CAP_BgPaper_e.pdf

Congress of Aboriginal Peoples. "Child Care Spaces Initiative." *ELCC Bulletin* No. 4 (Fall 2006).

Criminal Code, R.S.C. 1985, c. C-46.

Curry, Janet, C. *Best Practices: Treatment and Rehabilitation for Youth with Substance Use Problems*. Ottawa: Health Canada, 2001. Quoting Canadian Centre on Substance Abuse and Centre for Addiction and Mental Health, *Canadian Profile: Alcohol, Tobacco and Other Drugs*, Vols. 1997 and 1999. http://www.hc-sc.gc.ca/hl-vs/alt_formats/hecs-sesc/pdf/pubs/adp-apd/youth-jeunes/youth-jeunes_e.pdf

Dion Stout, Madeleine and Gregory D. Kipling. *Emerging Priorities for the Health of First Nations and Inuit Children and Youth*. Ottawa: First Nations and Inuit Health Branch (FNIHB), Health Canada, 1999. http://www.hc-sc.gc.ca/fnih-spni/pubs/develop/1999_priorit-child-enfant/index_e.html

Early Childhood Development Intercultural Partnerships. "Indigenous Fatherhood Project: Project Background." Victoria: Early Childhood Development Intercultural Partnerships, University of Victoria, 2007. http://www.ecdip.org/fathers/index.htm

Edmonton Joint Planning Committee on Housing. *A Count of Homeless Persons in Edmonton: October, 2004*. Edmonton: Edmonton Joint Planning Committee on Housing, undated. http://www.moresafehomes.net/HCReport2004.pdf

Environics Research Group. *2004 Baseline Study Among First Nations On-reserve and Inuit in the North*. Quoted in Health Canada, "Tobacco: Facts on Smoking Rates," Ottawa: Health Canada, 2005. http://www.hc-sc.gc.ca/fnih-spni/substan/tobac-tabac/index_e.html#facts

Eshkakogan, Nicole. "Young Aboriginal Women Missing: Who Cares?" AYN News, April 1, 2003. http://www.ayn.ca/ViewNews.aspx?id=267

Federal-Provincial-Territorial (FPT) Directors of Income Support. *Social Assistance Statistical Report: 2005*. Ottawa: Human Resources and Social Development Canada, 2006. http://www.hrsdc.gc.ca/en/cs/sp/sdc/socpol/publications/reports/sd10-3-2004e/page00.shtml

First Nations Child and Family Caring Society of Canada. *Non Discrimination and Diversity*. Submission to the United Nations Committee on the Rights of the Child. August 29, 2003. http://www.fncfcs.com/docs/UnitedNationsMay2004.pdf

Fontaine, Phil. "The Native Fiscal Imbalance." *The Globe and Mail*, October 30, 2006, p. A19.

Gough, P. et al. *Pathways to the Overrepresentation of Aboriginal Children in Care*. CECW Information Sheet #23E. Toronto: University of Toronto, 2005. www.cecw-cepb.ca/files/file/en/AboriginalChildren23E.pdf

Gough, P., C. Blackstock, and N. Bala. *Jurisdiction and funding models for Aboriginal child and family service agencies*. CECW Information Sheet #30E. Toronto: University of Toronto, 2005. http://www.cecw-cepb.ca/files/file/en/JurisdictionandFunding30E.pdf

Hallet, Bruce. *Aboriginal Peoples in Manitoba*. Winnipeg: Service Canada, 2006. http://www1.servicecanada.gc.ca/en/mb/aboriginal-profile/aboriginals.pdf

Health Canada. *A Second Diagnostic on the Health of First Nations and Inuit People in Canada*. Ottawa: Health Canada, 1999.

Health Canada. *A Statistical Profile on the Health of First Nations in Canada*. Ottawa: Health Canada, 2002.

Health Canada. "Suicide Prevention: Facts on Suicide Rates." Ottawa: Health Canada, 2003. http://www.hc-sc.gc.ca/fnih-spni/promotion/suicide/index_e.html

Health Canada. *Health Sectoral Session: Background Paper*. Ottawa: Government of Canada, 2004. http://www.aboriginalroundtable.ca/sect/hlth/bckpr/HC_BgPaper_e.pdf

Health Canada. "Early Childhood Development Strategy for Aboriginal Children: Expansion of Aboriginal Head Start (AHS)." Ottawa: Health Canada, 2005. http://www.hc-sc.gc.ca/fnih-spni/famil/develop/ahs-papa_expansion_e.html

Health Canada. "Statistical Profile on the Health of First Nations in Canada: Highlights of First Nations Health Statistics." Ottawa: Health Canada, 2005. http://www.hc-sc.gc.ca/fnih-spni/pubs/gen/stats_profil_e.html

Health Canada. "HIV and AIDS: Facts on HIV and AIDS in First Nations and Inuit Populations." Ottawa: Health Canada, 2006. http://www.hc-sc.gc.ca/fnih-spni/diseases-maladies/aids-sida/index_e.html

Health Canada. "Diabetes: Aboriginal Diabetes Initiative." Ottawa: Health Canada, 2007. http://www.hc-sc.gc.ca/fnih-spni/diseases-maladies/diabete/index_e.html

Health Canada. "Drinking water advisories." Ottawa: Health Canada, 2007. http://www.hc-sc.gc.ca/fnih-spni/promotion/water-eau/advis-avis_concern_e.html

Heisz, Andrew and Logan McLeod. *Low Income in Census Metropolitan Areas, 1980-2000*. Ottawa: Statistics Canada, 2004. Statistics Canada Catalogue no. 89-613-MIE. http://www.statcan.ca/english/research/89-613-MIE/89-613-MIE2004001.htm

Hull, Jeremy. *Aboriginal Single Mothers in Canada, 1996: A Statistical Profile*. Ottawa: Indian and Northern Affairs Canada, 2001. http://www.ainc-inac.gc.ca/pr/ra/smt/index_e.html

Hull, Jeremy. *Post-Secondary Education and Labour Market Outcomes: Canada, 2001*. Ottawa: Indian and Northern Affairs Canada, 2005. http://www.ainc-inac.gc.ca/pr/ra/pse/01/01_e.pdf

Hull, Jeremy. *Aboriginal Women: A Profile from the 2001 Census*. Ottawa: Indian and Northern Affairs Canada, 2006. http://www.ainc-inac.gc.ca/pr/pub/abw/abw_e.pdf

Human Resources and Skills Development Canada. *Canadian Youth: Who are they and what do they want*? Gatineau, Quebec : Human Resources and Skills Development Canada, 2005. http://www.youth.gc.ca/yoaux.jsp?&lang=en&flash=1&ta=1&auxpageid=846

Indian Act, R.S.C. 1985, c.I-5.

Indian and Northern Affairs Canada (INAC). *Canada-Aboriginal Peoples Roundtable: Lifelong Learning Background Paper.* Ottawa: Government of Canada, 2004. http://aboriginalroundtable.ca/sect/lrng/bckpr/INAC_BgPaper_LLL1_2_e.pdf

INAC. *Basic Departmental Data 2003.* Ottawa: INAC, 2004. http://www.ainc-inac.gc.ca/pr/sts/bdd03/bdd03_e.pdf

INAC. *Basic Departmental Data 2004.* Ottawa: INAC, 2005. http://www.ainc-inac.gc.ca/pr/sts/bdd04/bdd04_e.pdf

INAC. "Fact Sheet: Aboriginal Housing." Ottawa: INAC, 2006. http://www.ainc-inac.gc.ca/pr/info/fnsocec/abhsg_e.html

INAC. "Income Assistance Reform—The Way Forward." Ottawa: INAC, [n.d].

Indigenous Network on Economics and Trade (INET), et al. *Independent Indigenous Submission to the United Nations Committee on Economic, Social and Cultural Rights in Response to Canada's Periodic Reports.* Joint Submission to the United Nations Committee on Economic, Social and Cultural Rights, 36th Session. May 2006. http://www.ohchr.org/english/bodies/cescr/docs/info-ngos/independentindigenous.pdf

Inuit Tapiriit Kanatami (ITK). *Backgrounder on Inuit and Education.* Ottawa: ITK, 2004. http://www.aboriginalroundtable.ca/sect/lrng/bckpr/ITK_BgPaper_LLL1_2_e.pdf

ITK. *Backgrounder on Inuit and Housing.* Ottawa: ITK, 2004. http://www.aboriginalroundtable.ca/sect/hsng/bckpr/ITK_BgPaper_e.pdf

ITK. *Backgrounder on Inuit Health.* Ottawa: ITK, 2004. http://www.aboriginalroundtable.ca/sect/hlth/bckpr/ITK_BgPaper_e.pdf

Latimer, Jeff and Laura Casey Foss. *A One-Day Snapshot of Aboriginal Youth in Custody Across Canada: Phase II.* Ottawa: Department of Justice Canada, 2004. http://justice-canada.net/en/ps/rs/rep/2004/snap2/snapshot2.pdf

Ledrou, Ingrid and Jean Gervais. "Food Insecurity." *Health Reports.* 16, 3 (May 2005): 47-51. Statistics Canada Catalogue no. 82-003. http://www.statcan.ca/english/freepub/82-003-XIE/0030482-003-XIE.pdf

MacDonald, Nancy and Judy MacDonald. "Reflections of a Mi'kmaq social worker on a quarter of a century work in First Nations child welfare." *First Peoples Child and Family Review* 3, 1 (2007): 34-45. http://www.fncfcs.com/pubs/vol3num1/MacDonald_MacDonald_pp34.pdf

Mann, Michelle M. *Aboriginal Women: An Issues Backgrounder.* Ottawa: Status of Women Canada, 2005. http://www.swc-cfc.gc.ca/resources/consultations/ges09-2005/aboriginal_e.pdf

Maxim, Paul and Jerry White. "School Completion and Workforce Transitions." In *Aboriginal Policy Research: Moving Forward Making a Difference (Volume III),* edited by Jerry P. White, Paul Maxim and Dan Beavon. Toronto: Thompson Educational Publishing Inc., 2006.

McHardy, Mindy and Erin O'Sullivan. *First Nations Community Well-Being in Canada: The Community Well-Being Index (CWB) 2001.* Ottawa: Indian and Northern Affairs Canada, 2004. http://www.ainc-inac.gc.ca/pr/ra/cwb/cwb_e.pdf

McIvor et al. v. The Registrar, Indian and Northern Affairs Canada et al., 2007 BCSC 26 (CanLII).

Mendelson, Michael. *Aboriginal Peoples and Postsecondary Education in Canada.* Ottawa: Caledon Institute of Social Policy, 2006. http://www.caledoninst.org/Publications/PDF/595ENG.pdf

Mendelson, Michael. *Improving Primary and Secondary Education on Reserves in Canada.* Ottawa: Caledon Institute of Social Policy, 2006. http://www.caledoninst.org/Publications/PDF/608ENG.pdf

Metcalfe, Laura. *Exploring Empowering Education for Marginalized Youth in Toronto.* Toronto: For Youth Initiative, 2003. http://www.foryouth.ca/resources/downloads/empowering_report.pdf

National Aboriginal Health Organization (NAHO), "First Nations Center Survey of Youth Health Issues and Priorities," accessed August 8, 2007. http://www.naho.ca/firstnations/english/nations_circle_reports_stats.php

Native Council of Canada. *Native Child Care: the Circle of Care.* Ottawa: Native Council of Canada, 1990.

National Council of Welfare. *Justice and the Poor.* Ottawa: Public Works and Government Services Canada, 2000. http://www.ncwcnbes.net/en/publications/pub-111.html

National Council of Welfare. *Welfare Incomes 2005.* Ottawa: Public Works and Government Services Canada, 2006. http://www.ncwcnbes.net/en/publications/pub-125.html

National Council of Welfare. *Poverty Profile, 2002 and 2003.* Ottawa: Public Works and Government Services Canada, 2006. http://www.ncwcnbes.net/en/publications/pub-124.html

National Council of Welfare. *Solving Poverty: Four Cornerstones of a Workable National Strategy for Canada*. Ottawa: Public Works and Government Services Canada, 2007. http://www.ncwcnbes.net/en/publications/pub-126.html

Norris, Mary Jane. "Aboriginal Languages in Canada: Trends and Perspectives on Maintenance and Revitalization." In *Aboriginal Policy Research: Moving Forward Making a Difference (Volume III)*, edited by Jerry P. White, Paul Maxim and Dan Beavon. Toronto: Thompson Educational Publishing, 2006.

Norris, Mary Jane and Stewart Clatworthy. "Aboriginal Mobility and Migration in Canada: Factors, Policy Implications and Responses." Presentation to the Aboriginal Policy Research Conference. Ottawa, March 21-23, 2006. http://sociology.uwo.ca/aprc-crmpa/UPDATED%20MJ%20Norris%20APRC%20Migration%20Mar%2021%202006.swf

North-South Partnership for Children, Mamow Sha-way-gi-kay-win. "Immediate Action Needed to Aid First Nation Communities". Sandy Lake First Nation, ON: North-South Partnership for Children, June 26, 2007. http://www.northsouthpartnership.com/PressReleaseJune26.pdf

OECD. *Starting Strong II: Early Childhood Education and Care*. Paris: OECD Publications, 2006.

Office of the Correctional Investigator (OCI). *Annual Report of the Office of the Correctional Investigator 2005-2006*. Ottawa: Minister of Public Works and Government Services Canada, 2006. http://www.oci-bec.gc.ca/reports/AR200506_download_e.asp

OCI. "Backgrounder: Aboriginal Inmates." Ottawa: OCI, 2006. http://www.oci-bec.gc.ca/newsroom/bk-AR0506_e.asp

OCI. "Report Finds Evidence of Systemic Discrimination Against Aboriginal Inmates in Canada's Prisons." Ottawa: OCI, October 16, 2006. www.oci-bec.gc.ca/newsroom/releases/20061016_e.asp

Pauktuutit Inuit Women of Canada. *The Inuit Way: A Guide to Inuit Culture*. Ottawa: Pauktuutit Inuit Women of Canada, 2006. http://www.pauktuutit.ca/pdf/publications/pauktuutit/InuitWay_e.pdf

Pauktuutit Inuit Women of Canada. *Issue Paper: Poverty*. For the National Aboriginal Women's Summit. [N.p.]: Pauktuutit Inuit Women of Canada, 2007. http://www.laa.gov.nl.ca/laa/naws/pdf/Poverty.pdf

Richard, K. "A commentary against Aboriginal to non-Aboriginal adoption." *First Peoples Child and Family Review* 1, 1 (September 2004): 101-109. http://www.fncfcs.com/pubs/vol1num1/Richard_pp101-109.pdf

Roy, Jennifer. "Acknowledging Racism." [N.p.]: Canadian Race Relations Foundation, [n.d.]. http://www.crr.ca/divers-files/en/pub/faSh/ePubFaShAckRac.pdf

Social Planning and Research Council of BC. "On our streets and in our shelters... Results of the 2005 Greater Vancouver Homeless Count - Bulletin." Vancouver: Social Planning and Research Council of BC, 2005. http://www.gvrd.bc.ca/homelessness/pdfs/HomelessCount2005Bulletin.pdf

Statistics Canada. *Aboriginal Peoples of Canada: A Demographic Profile*. Analysis Series, 2001 Census. Ottawa: Statistics Canada, 2003. Catalogue no. 96F0030XIE2001007. http://www12.statcan.ca/english/census01/products/analytic/companion/abor/pdf/96F0030XIE2001007.pdf

Statistics Canada. "Aboriginal Peoples Survey: Well-being of the non-reserve Aboriginal population." *The Daily*. Ottawa: Statistics Canada, September 24, 2003. Catalogue no. 11-001-XIE. http://www.statcan.ca/Daily/English/030924/d030924.pdf

Statistics Canada. *Education in Canada: Raising the standard*. Analysis Series, 2001 Census. Ottawa: Statistics Canada, 2003. Catalogue no. 96F0030XIE2001012. http://www12.statcan.ca/english/census01/Products/Analytic/companion/educ/pdf/96F0030XIE2001012.pdf

Statistics Canada. *Selected Labour Force Characteristics (50), Aboriginal Identity (8), Age Groups (5A), Sex (3) and Area of Residence (7) for Population 15 Years and Over, for Canada, Provinces and Territories, 2001 Census—20% Sample Data* (table). *Topic-based tabulations: Aboriginal Peoples of Canada*. Ottawa: Statistics Canada, November 19, 2003. 2001 Census of Canada. Catalogue No. 97F0011XCB2001044.

Statistics Canada. *Selected Income Characteristics (35A), Aboriginal Identity (8), Age Groups (6), Sex (3) and Area of Residence (7) for Population, for Canada, Provinces and Territories, 2001 Census—20% Sample Data* (table). *Topic-based tabulations: Aboriginal Peoples of Canada*. Ottawa: Statistics Canada, December 10, 2003. 2001 Census of Canada. Catalogue No. 97F0011XCB2001046.

Statistics Canada. *Selected Income Characteristics (35), Registered Indian Status (3), Age Groups (6) and Sex(3) for Population, for Canada, Provinces, Territories and Census Metropolitan Areas, 2001 Census—20% Sample Data* (table). *Topic-based tabulations: Aboriginal Peoples of Canada*. Ottawa: Statistics Canada, March 24, 2004. 2001 Census of Canada. Catalogue No. 97F0011XCB2001063.

Statistics Canada. *Family Income Groups(21),Sex(3) and Aboriginal Group of Lone Parent(11) for Lone-parent Census Families in Private Households,for Canada, Provinces and Territories, 2000—20% Sample Data* (table). *Topic-based tabulations: Income of Individuals, Families and Households*. Ottawa: Statistics Canada, June 16, 2004. 2001 Census of Canada. Catalogue No. 97F0020XCB2001065.

Statistics Canada. *A Profile of Canada's Métis Population*. Ottawa: Statistics Canada, 2004. http://www.aboriginalroundtable.ca/sect/stscan/Metis_e.pdf

Statistics Canada. *A Profile of Canada's Inuit Population.* Ottawa: Statistics Canada, 2004. http://www.aboriginalroundtable.ca/sect/stscan/Inuit_e.pdf

Statistics Canada. *The Canadian Labour Market at a Glance, 2005.* Ottawa: Statistics Canada, 2006. Catalogue No. 71-222-XIE. http://www.statcan.ca/english/freepub/71-222-XIE/71-222-XIE2006001.pdf

Statistics Canada. *Projections of the Aboriginal populations, Canada, provinces and territories: 2001 to 2017.* Ottawa: Statistics Canada, 2005. Catalogue no. 91-547-XIE. http://www.statcan.ca/english/freepub/91-547-XIE/91-547-XIE2005001.pdf

Statistics Canada. *Measuring Violence Against Women: Statistical Trends 2006.* Ottawa: Statistics Canada, 2006. Catalogue no. 85-570-XIE. http://www.statcan.ca/english/research/85-570-XIE/85-570-XIE2006001.pdf

Statistics Canada. *Income Trends in Canada 1980-2005* [CD-ROM]. Ottawa: Statistics Canada, 2007. Catalogue no. 13F0022XIE.

Statistics Canada. *Population Reporting an Aboriginal Identity, by Age Group, by Province and Territory (2001 Census)* (table). *Summary Tables.* http://www.statcan.ca/l01/cst01/demo40a.htm?sdi=aboriginal%20identity

Statistics Canada. "Aboriginal Peoples of Canada: Definitions." Ottawa: Statistics Canada, [n.d.]. http://www12.statcan.ca/english/census01/Products/Analytic/companion/abor/definitions.cfm

The Canada Gazette. Part III. Vol. 29, No. 2 (31 January 2007).

The Constitution Act, 1867 (U.K.), 30 & 31 Victoria, c. 3.

The Constitution Act, 1982, being Schedule B to the *Canada Act 1982* (U.K.), 1982, c. 11.

Trevethan, Shelley, et al. *The Needs of Inuit Offenders in Federal Correctional Facilities.* Ottawa: Correctional Service of Canada, 2004. http://www.csc-scc.gc.ca/text/rsrch/reports/r142/r142_e.shtml

Turcotte, Martin and Grant Schellenberg. *A Portrait of Seniors in Canada.* Ottawa: Statistics Canada, 2007. Statistics Canada Catalogue no. 89 519-XPE. http://www.statcan.ca/english/freepub/89-519-XIE/89-519-XIE2006001.pdf

Wurm, Stephen, ed. *Atlas of the World's Languages in Danger of Disappearing.* Paris: UNESCO, 1996.

Youth Criminal Justice Act, S.C. 2002, c. 1.

CREDITS/ABOUT THE NATIONAL COUNCIL OF WELFARE

MEMBERS

Dr. John Rook *(Chairperson)—Calgary, Alberta*

Angela Cormier—*Wellington, Prince Edward Island*

Greg deGroot-Maggetti—*Kitchener, Ontario*

James Hughes—*Montréal, Québec*

Gail MacDougall—*Halifax, Nova Scotia*

Ronald Murray—*Fredericton, New Brunswick*

Sonia Racine—*Québec, Québec*

Dr. Joseph Tietz—*Vancouver, British Columbia*

David Welch—*Ottawa, Ontario*

MEMBERS, SUB-COMMITTEE—ABORIGINAL PROJECT (2005/2006)

Hope Hunter—*Edmonton, Alberta*

Allyce Herle—*Regina, Saskatchewan*

Josie Hill—*Winnipeg, Manitoba*

David Welch—*Ottawa, Ontario*

Dr. David Newhouse *(advisor to the NCW),
Department of Native Studies,
Trent University*

STAFF

Director: **Sheila Regehr**

Senior Researcher and Policy Advisor: **Cathy Oikawa**

Researcher and Policy Advisor: **Diane Richard**

Research Assistant: **Musarrat Rana**

Administration and Information Officer: **Carrie-Ann Breckenridge**

Administrative Assistant: **Claudette Mann**

Contractor/Writer for this Aboriginal report: **Michelle M. Mann,**
*is a Toronto-based lawyer, writer and consultant who practiced law for
several years and is former legal counsel to the federal Department of
Justice and the Indian Claims Commission. She has authored many
reports and book chapters on Aboriginal, gender and human rights
issues.*

REVIEWERS

Sarah Carrière, *Inuit Tapiriit Kanatami*

Jennifer Dickson, *Executive Director, Pauktuutit Inuit Women of Canada*

Rosalinda Costa, *Analyst, Aboriginal Data Initiative, Statistics Canada*

Lorraine Foreman, *Director of Operations, Congress of Aboriginal Peoples*

Alfred J. Gay, *Policy Analyst, National Association of Friendship Centres*

Dr. Valerie Gideon, *Senior Director, Health and Social Secretariat, Assembly of First Nations*

Josie Hill, *Former Member of the NCW / Executive Director, Ma Mawi Wi Chi Itata Centre*

Hope Hunter, *Former Member of the NCW / Executive Director, Boyle Street Community Services*

Soha Kneen, *Senior Researcher/Operations Manager, Environment, Inuit Tapiriit Kanatami*

Heidi Langille, *Coordinator, Early Learning and Child Care, Pauktuutit Inuit Women of Canada*

Sherry Lewis, *Executive Director, Native Women's Association of Canada*

Dr. David Newhouse, *Chair and Associate Professor, Indigenous Studies, and Associate Professor, Business Administration, Trent University*

Heather Tait, *Project Advisor, Inuit Information, Environment and Health Department, Inuit Tapiriit Kanatami*

Eleanor M. Thomas, *Senior Analyst, Special Surveys Division, Statistics Canada*

Barbara Van Haute, *Associate Director of Health, Métis National Council*

Nancy Zukewich, *Senior Analyst, Aboriginal Data Initiative, Statistics Canada*

RESEARCHERS
(2005/2006)

John Anderson, *NCW (played an instrumental role, especially in organizing the interviews for this report.)*

Lucie Cossette, *NCW*

Matthew Sanger, *NCW*

Trica McDiarmid, *Research Contractor (Port Coquitlam, British Columbia)*

NATIONAL COUNCIL OF WELFARE— ABORIGINAL RESEARCH ROUNDTABLE ON POVERTY (2005)

PARTICIPANTS

John Anderson, *Vice-President, Strategic Partnerships and Alliances, Canadian Council on Social Development*

Linda Borden, *NCW Member—Newfoundland and Labrador*

Angela Cormier, *NCW Member—Prince Edward Island*

Lucie Cossette, *NCW Researcher, Aboriginal Project*

Greg deGroot-Maggetti, *NCW Member—Ontario*

Peter Dinsdale, *Executive Director, National Association of Friendship Centres*

Kowesa Etitiq, *Senior Project Coordinator, Inuit Tapiriit Kanatami*

Alfred Gay, *Policy Analyst, National Association of Friendship Centres*

Anne Gill, *NCW Member—Northwest Territories*

Christopher Googoo, *Commercial Account Manager, Ulnooweg Development Group*

Wayne Helgason, *Executive Director, Social Planning Council of Winnipeg*

Allyce Herle, *NCW Member—Saskatchewan*

Josephine Hill, *NCW Member—Manitoba*

Maggie Hodgson (Hon), *Advisor Residential Schools, Edmonton*

James Hughes, *NCW Member—Quebec*

Hope Hunter, *NCW Member—Alberta*

Laurie Kilpatrick, *NCW Director*

Ida Labillois-Montour, *President, Native Women's Shelter of Montreal*

John Murphy, *NCW Chairperson*

Ronald Murray, *NCW Member—New-Brunswick*

Dr. David Newhouse, *Trent University*

Melinda Norris, *NCW Note-taker/Reporter*

Cathy Oikawa, *NCW Senior Researcher and Policy Advisor*

Marie Patry, *Coordinator, Aboriginal Data Initiative, Statistics Canada*

Sonia Racine, *NCW Member—Quebec*

Kenn Richard, *Executive Director, Native Child and Family Services of Toronto*

Paul E. Skanks, *Elder*

Adeline Webber, *President, Whitehorse Aboriginal Women's Circle*

David Welch, *NCW Member—Ontario*

Valorie Whetung, *Senior Advisor, Social and Aboriginal Statistics, Division, Statistics Canada*

MANDATE OF THE NATIONAL COUNCIL OF WELFARE

The National Council of Welfare was established by the *Government Organization Act* in 1969, as an arm's length advisory body to the federal government. It advises the Minister of Human Resources and Social Development on matters of concern to low-income Canadians.

The Council consists of members drawn from across Canada and appointed by the Governor-in-Council. All members serve in their personal capacities rather than as representatives of organizations or agencies. Council membership over the years has reflected expertise in a wide range of social development and social security issues. Members have also reflected varied backgrounds, from education and social work to voluntary sector organization and policy analysis, including experience living in poverty.

Reports by the National Council of Welfare deal with a wide range of issues on poverty and social policy in Canada, including income security programs, welfare reform, medicare, poverty lines and poverty statistics, the retirement income system, taxation, labour market issues, social services and legal aid.

Pour vous procurer des exemplaires en français de publications du Conseil, écrivez au Conseil national du bien-être social, 9e étage, 112, rue Kent, Ottawa (Ontario) K1A 0J9. Vous pouvez les demander par courrier électronique ncw@magi.com ou les consulter sur notre site web www.ncwcnbes.net.